MEMOIRS OF A TELEPHONE MAN

BILL BAILEY

Print ISBN: 978-1-66783-985-1
eBook ISBN: 978-1-66783-986-8

About The Author

William H. Bailey Jr. was born in Boston and raised in Dorchester, Massachusetts. In high school, he was the lead singer of a band and won a variety competition in Charlestown, Massachusetts. After graduation, he worked at some well-known companies like General Electric, and Westinghouse Electric, until finally working for the New England Tell Telephone Company in his mid-twenties. Since then, the phone company has change names a few times and is now Verizon. William or Bill as his friends call him, has worked in many departments in the phone company, from Central Office Equipment Installation, to working in an office as a service order writer for A T& T Long lines, then to the Coin Department, being a coin collector, to a coin repairman, and then a resident and business repairman, to being in the Cable Department when he retired, with thirty-two years of service. Most of those years was spent as a Telephone repairman technician, and that's where the adventures began.

Since retiring, he would see different things that reminded him a lot of the repair jobs he had over the years. He could be at home watching television with family and something would come on that reminded him of a customer he had. When he would tell friends and family about the encounters he had, the people every time would say "you know you should write a book" At the movies, he would mention to his friends about something on the screen that was familiar to him at a customer's house years ago. Just walking down the street, he would tell who he was with about a repair that happened in a certain residence or business they would be walking by, and the people kept telling Bill, "you need to put that in a book because the adventures you have had over the years going to different people's homes would make very interesting reading".

He repaired and brought service to poor people on welfare, to the super rich. He has met people in every economical walk of life, and most were friendly and kind. It took years to complete the book. After writing a couple of chapters, he put the book on the back burner to pursue a singing career after recording a CD. Entitled SONGS I GREW UP TO, which sold around the world on the internet website CD BABY. COM. Oldies music from the fifties and sixties, and then moved to Las Vegas where he put together an oldies tribute show. When the pandemic hit the world, all entertainment in Las Vegas stopped, had he was able to refocus on the book. Every word is true and the people, places and things he went through are all real.

Acknowledgments

I want to thank my mother and father, coming from Virginia to Boston, Massachusetts in the 1940's they worked hard. My father William Henry Bailey Sr., was in World War II, he boxed in the Army. He was also a drummer, a barber and a tap dancer in show business in the 1950's. He worked three jobs to support us. My mother Adeana Bailey, worked as a tailor. My parents taught me about work ethics, and that stuck with me all these years. My Mother made sure we went to church every Sunday, so I would know the Lord. She also taught me right from wrong, and to treat other people the way I would want to be treated. She also told me to never put people down, but instead to up lift people and help when I can. Another person I would like to address is a fellow telephone man Donald Brady, we were good friends in Brockton, Massachusetts. This is someone I knew for over fifty years; he joined the company after I did. I just want him to be remembered he passed way February 10, 2021.

Chapter 1

THE ATTACK CAT

It was in the middle of the day I got a repair call to go to a rooming house. It was a three-story building I was told from dispatch to go to the landlady on the first floor and I rang her bell, telephone company, l, said as she answered the door. Good she said MISS JOHNSON is expecting you, she's at work but I'll let you in. The landlady was a middle-aged woman, small in stature, and she had the keys in her hand. Follow me she said, as we went to the back apartment, which was on the same floor. As we got to the door, she said MISS JOHNSON has a cat and we have to make sure it doesn't get out.

I never go in her apartment and I hardly ever see her but. hear from the other tenants there's something wrong with the cat. So, I thought to myself it's only a cat it's not like she has a pit bull in there. As she opens the door, I can smell the odor of a cat. The room was dimly lit from the sunlight coming in the room from the back window. She shut the door behind us and I heard the latch lock. It was a medium kitchenette. With a small bedroom on the left side a very large worn red couch in the middle of the room with a foot stool and an end table that held the lamp that the land lady turned on. I could hear the big clock on the wall ticking the seconds away, there's the phone over there she said it was on another end table on the other side of the couch. I went over and picked the phone up yep, no dial tone. I said and started to trace the cord going to the phone jack which was near the back window. All of sudden, in the shadows, there was something moving on the floor and moving fast it was circling the room. I saw glimpses of it when the light hit it but it mostly ran around the room in the shadows. The landlady started screaming, and SHOUTED WHAT IS THAT? I saw it in the light as it was trying to gain altitude, a large Angora cat, it jumped from the floor to the foot stool to the back of the couch and leaped at me with all its claws pointed at my head. I ducked, and it went right over my shoulders. Are you kidding me? I've never seen anything like this a house cat, the landlady was still screaming as she grabbed the broom. It was still moving. The cat then went from the floor to the end table and leaped at her, she was swinging that broom like WILLY MAYS.

The landlady was screaming open the bathroom door! open the bathroom door! I jumped across the room like CARL LEWIS. I open the door as she corralled the cat with the broom into the bathroom. We both slammed the door and was leaning on it, out of breath looking at each other, as if we had just made it into the house as we ran from a serial killer. The first thing out of her mouth was, that woman and that cat has got to go! She can't be in my apartment building with a dangerous animal, I almost had a heart attack she said. I kind of giggled to myself, and then said wow I have never seen a house cat act like that are you alright? She said yes, lock the door when your finished just make sure you shut the door. Whatever you do, don't let that damn cat out the bathroom! I am going to give her a piece of my mind when she comes home about that cat. Okay, I said and began to trace the phone wire IW. (inside wire) and found that it was broke at the window where it came into the apartment from the pole. I fixed it at the window and left. The whole job took about an hour and a half because of the cat drama, and oh what a drama that was!

Chapter 2

MAN WITH A GUN

I had an order for a luxury complex on Mass. Ave in Boston MA. It was a grey building which looked like it was part of the great Boston city hospital that everybody ended up going to sooner or later if you grew up in Boston. But It was two separate buildings, I rang the doorbell and over the Intercom a husky deep voice said who Is it and I said the phone company then he said get up here now I am In apt. 606 which knew from my work order. So took the elevator up to the six floor It smell kind of pleasant compared to the smell of the elevators in some projects. This part of town was between the two-man area which is Roxbury and the South End that [s a one-man area. Wherever there is a high crime area they put two men In the phone truck for safety. When you knock on a door you never know what to expect, and this is one of those times when you say to yourself WHAT THE F%@K. He opened the door with a gun in his hand pointing it right at me. I froze, put my hands in the air slightly bent and said whoa! Telephone man and I am here to help you to put you back in service. He was about six feet three and about 250 lbs. He waved me in with the gun and said close the door as he lowered the gun, he said he has been using his neighbor's phone and that he was very pissed off with the phone company. Now remember this was well before cellphones, he said he had been talking back and forth with the phone company and they were giving him the run around. He had called the business office for two weeks and they kept telling him his dial tone will be back on and nothing was happening. You see his mother was very sick and dying back in Africa where he was from and he couldn't get in touch with anybody back there because his phone was off. For two weeks he's been cussing out everybody in the business office because according to him nothings being done. So, he was on his way down to the business office to SHOOT all the service reps. Well, I said put the gun away and that I understand how he felt, I am on your side I am going to fix the problem. He had a nice apartment with modern furniture I went over to the phone there was no dial tone so what we normally do Is put my buzzer on his phone Jack and trace It down to the phone terminal to see if there is a clear signal to the terminal which In this case was In the basement sometimes It's on a pole. Also, to determine if the dial tone is coming Into the building. Before left his apartment he said I shouldn't let you leave before my phone Is fixed, but I assured him I had to go to the basement to see where the problem was and that my buzzer was there on his phone jack so I'll be back. But when I got to the basement the door for that part of the basement where the utility room was In was LOCKED, and there was a sign that said maintance will not be back until Monday and this was a Saturday. There was no way I was going back up to that guy's apartment to tell him I couldn't fix his phone he could keep the buzzer I had already determine that the problem was not in his apartment. I left the building and called dispatch and told them what the problem was they called the contact number for the building maintenance and there was no answer I told them that whoever they send out on this repair job to beware of the man with a gun.

Chapter 3

THE PATCH

I was in the telephone garage when I picked up my first job of the day from dispatch. I had To go on the other end of Massachusetts Avenue, heading towards Cambridge, across from Berkley School of music. It was a large apartment building a half a block long, eight floors, and about ten apartments on each floor with different stores on the ground floor. It's always hard to find a park on Massachusetts Avenue but I got one right in front of the main door to the building. I grabbed my tools and went over to the doorbells. The repair order said Smith 510#, I rang the bell the intercom. Had a lot of static but, I heard a lady's soft voice say who is it? I replied Telephone Man. Oh I have been waiting for you come on up. Now at this point, I had a choice either go down to the basement to the phone terminal to see if the dial tone was Coming into the building, or go upstairs to see if the problem was in the IW (inside wiring) in the apartment.

I knocked at the door, she opens the door and I saw she was a cute average size African American lady with Daisey dukes on. She said my phone has been out of service for three or four days and it's a Necessity that my phone stay on. I told her well, I am here to help you. Her apartment was laid out really nice with new furniture. She told me I was glad the intercom worked because sometimes you can't hear the person talking and the building maintenance was supposed to fix it weeks ago, I told her, but your phone will be fix before I leave, then she asked me would you like some water, soda or beer I said no I'm good as I was picking up a desk phone to check for dial tone. Most of the time the main wire coming from the phone terminal in the basement up through the building goes right into the kitchen phone on the wall but not all the time. It also can go to a phone jack along the baseboard near the floor. The problem with that, is there can be two or three jacks in each room so I spend a lot of time on my knees at each jack looking for the main feed coming up from the terminal. She told me she was desperate to get her phone fixed, so she had open up a couple of jacks, and I could see the wires were not put back on the jacks right, so I thought that was going to be an easy fix but I could see the problem was not at the jacks because there was no dial tone.

While down on my knees rewiring one of the jacks, I looked up and said I notice you're wearing a patch, did something get in your eye? What she said next blew my mind. She said, I was shot in the eye. Oh my, wow, what happen? She told me her and a boyfriend went to California on a vacation and to check it out. They were having a good time going different places exploring the West Coast, but then after a while they started arguing and not getting along. So, he took off and she was by herself for a while she didn't know if he had gone back to Boston or where he was. Then she told me, I had to get out and socialize and meet people so she met another man.

Now I'm listening to her and I am kind of taking my time, putting the wires and jacks back on the baseboard, because I wanted her to finish telling me how she got her eye shot out and why she isn't dead. After meeting this new guy, she brought him back to where she was staying. At this point I said to myself oh, oh I know where this is going, it was getting late so they went to bed, she told me they made love and fell asleep. All of a sudden, she was awakened by a loud bang. Her boyfriend was standing over her with a gun in his hand, he had just shot the man lying beside her in the head, and without warning pointed the gun at her and pulled the trigger. WOW I looked at her I was in a shock speechless, then she went on when she was hit, she screamed then went silent and just laid there and didn't move. She wasn't dead but she knew if she had moved even a little, he would have shot her again. She could hear him grabbing some stuff in a hurry and went out the door, she told me she laid there for a while scared to move. I thought man was she lucky, she said when she turned her head to the man next to her, she couldn't see out of one eye and his face was covered in blood.

The pain was tremendous, there was blood everywhere, she managed to reach the phone and call 911 told them what happen where she was at and passed out. When she came to, she was in the hospital.

The doctors told her they got the bullet out but she would be blind in one eye. The cops came and told her the guy in the bed was dead when they got there, they got the description from her about her boyfriend and put out an A.P.B. for him and told her we'll get him he won't get away with this. So, she said when I got out of the hospital I quickly came back to Boston and got this apartment. WOW! I said, that's quite a story it's a miracle your still here. I said you must feel safe now that they got him. No, she said they never found him and some people have told her they saw him here in Boston. Really? I said to her in amazement, I was finishing up the phone jack contemplating and visualizing everything she just said when the doorbell rang. She went to the intercom and said hello there was no answer she said hello again no answer, then all of a sudden, she yelled in a very loud voice its him. WAIT, WHAT! I said as I am picking up my tools off the floor in a hurry trying to put them back in my tool pouch. She was running around in circles screaming from the living room to the bedroom through the kitchen. He's going to kill me! He's going to kill me! I scrambled to my feet; I was shaking so bad all my tools fell out my pouch back on the floor. All I knew was if that was him, he's not going to leave any witnesses, I have got to get OUT of here. At one point, while she was screaming, she said he's going to kill us. That's when some of my tools fell out again. Now I was trying to remain calm as I gathered up my tools, I calmly walked to the door and told her I think the problem is in the basement I'll call you in a few minutes, ignoring her going berserk right in front of me.

I WAS TRYING TO BE COOL. When I shut the door, I was so nervous ran to the elevators I did not want to run into him especially him seeing me coming out of her apartment. When I got to the terminal, I found some wires had come loose from her apartment going to the dial tone at the phone terminal in the basement. I got on another line to call her; I have to admit I was extremely nervous because I didn't know what to expect. The phone rang twice, she picked it up, with a pleasant voice and I thought to myself thank God she's okay. She went on to say, I haven't heard this phone ring in such a long time thank you very much for fixing it for me, then she said it was my father who rang the bell. He came to tell me they caught that fool who shot me. He tried to call but the phone was out, so thank you again! I told her I was glad everything worked out good for her. Now I'm not a scaredy cat, and I do know how to handle myself being a black belt in karate, but. It wasn't my beef, and I was just doing my job repairing her phone service, but if her boyfriend had come in while I was there, I would have had no choice but to protect her and myself at the best of my abilities. That was quite the experience that's why I'll never forget the lady with THE PATCH.

MAN ON POLE.

Chapter 4

THE SHADDUCK

In the telephone company, as a repair technician, I worked in two different departments which were the coin and residence which includes the businesses department. While I was in the coin department, my job was to repair payphones. This was before cell phones, which doesn't seem that long ago. Sometimes I had to go to the same building over and over again, because the payphones would go out of service at different times such as at the airport, a factory or a hospital, and they would have many payphones on different floors. One of these places was the Lemuel Shadduck Hospital in Mattapan, Boston, Massachusetts. Several floors had regular sick patients and some floors had specialty patients, which means the whole floor had one kind of sickness, and at the time I didn't know that. Now when I get a repair order from dispatch, all they give you is the name of the place, the address, the floor, and the phone number of the phone to be fixed. It was the middle of the day, and I had closed out a few jobs, when I got an order to go to the Shadduck Hospital.

Now this was my first time there, so as I was going through the lobby a security guard stopped me and asked, "where are you going?" I said, "phone company", I'm here to fix the payphone on the fourth floor. He said, "take the elevators on the right" and when I got off the elevator, I was in a hallway with a door straight ahead. I went over to the door, it was locked so I rang the bell, I thought it was a little strange that the door was locked to a hospital floor. I rang the bell again, and finally a nurse with a mask on opened the door. I showed her my tools, as I said phone company. said, "do you have a payphone out of order?" She said, "yes, come in", as she locked the door behind me. She led me down a long hall with rooms with beds in them, on each side. She showed me the phone and said, "I hope you can fix it, because this the only link some of the patients have to their families'. There is another payphone on the other side of the ward, but there is always a long line and the patients get frustrated. While I was taking the phone apart, and putting the parts on the floor, patients kept coming up one by one asking me when the phone was going to be fixed. Some of the patients started saying, hey I lost my money in that phone are you going to give it back to me? Of course, that was something that I was used to hearing when repairing a payphone, I would tell them, if you call the phone company and tell them what happen they will send you back the money you lost. People are always losing money in the payphones, especially when it's out of order. Now I was starting to notice everybody that came up to me had a mask on, the doctors had masks on, the nurses had masks on, and all the patients had masks on. I was working on that phone as fast as can, I knew something was wrong. I put the phone back together and hurried over to the Nurse's Station and asked how come everybody has a mask on? The nurses all looked up from their desks and one said, they didn't tell you this is a TUBERCULOSIS WARD. WHAT! No, I said as I was putting my shirt up over my nose like a mask. I did not get that information; I knew I had to get out of there! Normally you have to close out a job with dispatch from the phone you just fixed, so they can test the phone, and sometimes it takes a while, but I wasn't staying another minute on the T.B. WARD.

Over the years, I had got a number of repair orders for the Shadduck, and encountered different situations, and like I said, the orders never tell you what kind of medical procedure is done on each floor. I had repair jobs all over Boston, and surrounding towns, and about three months later, I got another order for the Shadduck but on a different floor. As I got off the elevator on the fifth floor, I walk over to a door which was locked. I said to myself, not again! So, I rang. the doorbell and knocked on the door twice I could see a nurse through the little glass window coming to the door. She didn't have a mask on. Oh good, I thought it's just a regular hospital ward. She let me in, and locked the door behind me. It was another long corridor with bedrooms on both sides. She showed me the payphone, and I started taking it apart There were patients once again coming up to me asking when it was going to be fixed and that they lost money in the phone. I told them what to do to get their money back. Nobody was wearing a mask, so I felt safe. As I was working, I notice one of the patients sauntered herself, real slow and sexy like, staring at me as she came over and put her arm on my shoulder. She said I know you; she was an average looking lady in the face with blonde hair but super skinny.

I said you know me from where? She said that she lives in the South End of Boston, and that she has seen me jogging around Black Stone Park. I did jog regularly there but I also jog around the Charles River, but at the time I lived in the South End. What a coincidence I said. I even spoke to you, and said hi, but you didn't notice me she said. I told her when I am jogging, I try to stay focus to get it over with. Then I said so, why are you at the Shadduck are you sick? Of course, I knew she had to be, but I was wondering what was wrong. Then she told me yes, I have AIDS FROM H.I.V. Then very calmly I said, I hope you get well soon, as I slowly tried to move away from her. Back then there was all kind of different rumors on how people got AIDS. I said I will pray for you, and she said thank you. This was an AIDS Ward, when I closed out the job with dispatch, I asked them why don't they tell us what kind of hospital ward they are sending us to? The answer is always the same, they are never given that information. I felt really bad for the lady, because back then AIDS was a death sentence.

Sometime later that year I got another repair order to go to the Shadduck Hospital. So, I asked dispatch, what kind of sickness would be on this ward I was going to, was it T.B. OR AIDS OR what? You see I was just trying to prepare myself beforehand so I knew what I was getting in to. All they knew was the payphone was on the top floor, so I went thru the Hospital Lobby, and said hi to the security guard and got on the elevator to the top floor, not knowing what to expect when I got off. When the elevator door opened, the hallway was the same as the other floors, but when I got to the door of the ward it was a very thick iron door with a little glass peep hole at the top. I rang the bell, but this time instead of a nurse opening the door, I heard a deep voice coming over an intercom, WHO IS IT WHAT DO YOU WANT? Telephone Company, I said, I am here to fix the payphone. The next thing I knew, the door opened and there was a prison guard standing in front of me behind another door with bars. Ok, I am thinking what kind of place this is, he opens the bars and let me in and said I'll have to search you. I had to step thru a metal detector and he patted me down. Alright, I said what is this place? The prison guard began to explain that when prisoners get real sick, they can't take them to a regular hospital, so the State had a facility built for them in a hospital. The prison guards keep an eye on them so they can't escape while they are being treated. I told him well that was a new one on me! I have never saw a prison in a hospital, he went on to tell me, you know it's like ten stories in this hospital, and most people that come into the building are not even aware that there is a prison up here. I thought of what he said, and he was right, who knew? Some of the patients were kind of wondering around, but I notice that on that floor rooms had bars on them. While I was fixing the payphone, a couple of the patients (prisoners) came up to me. But, instead of asking how they get their money back they lost in the phone, they were demanding I give it to them right there, but the prison guard was with me, and escorted them back to their cell. I repaired the phone and left; it was another amazing adventure at the SHADDOCK.

Chapter 5

DOGS

Like the mailman, the telephone repairman encounters a lot of dogs in his travels. However, there is a difference, the postman always runs into dogs outside either near the mailbox, or when he or she approaches the house. There could be a dog in the yard barking at them, or one straggling down the street, and the dog spots the mail person and decides to chase them to bite their leg off. Now for the telephone repairman, it's a whole different circumstance when you walk into a person's home. The dog knows it's his or her domain and will let you know it. Not all dogs are vicious, if the owner is right there, and some dogs are pretty friendly.

I have encountered all types, and here's one that comes to mind. I had a repair residential order not far from Chinatown and on this street all the buildings looked the same, only two floors and were joined together. I arrived at the address on the order grabbed my tool belt, from the truck and rang the doorbell, and a middle-aged man with a semi-bald head answered the door. I said, "telephone company" and he responded, "it's about time there was another repairman here yesterday and he didn't fix nothing and my phone is still out". I said, "I'm going to see what I can do to get you back in service". OH, and by the way this guy had two PIT BULLS in each hand by their collars, and the dogs were barking and snarling at me with drool coming out their mouths, and standing on their hind legs. I said to the guy, " listen, you have to put these dogs away or else I am not coming in". (l know about pit bulls, I had one for seven years. He wasn't your average forty pounder. He weighed 80 pounds, tall and all muscle. He looked like a body builder his name was Kojak.) Well, he put the dogs away in a room and closed the door but they were still barking like crazy.

He led me through the house to the backyard and said, "the other repairman was working on that box outside on the wall for a long time". As I was going through the house, I picked up one of the phones to check for dial tone there was none. When I got out to the backyard and to the phone terminal on the wall, I realized I was in a courtyard. All of these buildings were joined together with one big yard and a twenty-foot brick wall on the other side of the yard. There was only one way out of the yard and that was back through the customer's door. Before he closed his back door, he said, "I am not going to let you back in until my phone is fixed". Some phone terminals are on a pole, some in a basement, some in a regular yard on back of the house, and then there's the courtyard. I knew there was going to be a problem when I opened the terminal, traced his drop (wire) from his building, and found that his dial tone was not there. I called the Central Office from another line to get a spare pair to the terminal but there wasn't any. In a case like this, we would turn this repair order over to the Cable Department, and they would come out and go in the man whole in the street and fix the problem. Now the other repairman before me, saw this situation and knew what needed to be done, but for whatever reason it wasn't done. Now I am in a pickle, because the customer already told me he was not going to let me out of the courtyard until it's fixed. What to do, what to do, I had to think. I knew I had to get to my phone truck, I normally wear, my tool belt over my shoulder to me it's more comfortable but a lot of guys wear it around their waist. So, put it around my waist, my plan was to tell him have to get a special tool from my truck and I'll be right back. If the tool belt was around my shoulder, he might ask why are you taking your tools, just going to your truck? Normally, I would tell the customer the problem in in the manhole and the cable department is coming out to put you back in service, but this guy was already very angry.

I knocked on the back door, and he opened the door with the dogs by his side snarling and barking. I thought, "here we go again", and he said, "is it all set?" I was very careful with my words, I told him, "it will be just another two minutes there is a tool I need from my truck and you will be all set". He looked at me very steeled-eyed as he slowly backed up so I could come in. I walked at a fast pace through the house towards the front door, he was right on my heels with those dogs barking. I was nervous knowing that if he let go of the collars, these pits could grab my leg bite down and break bones. Most dogs don't have that kind of power. So, my truck was right outside his door he stood there watching me, dogs barking away. As I was walking to the truck, I had my keys in my hand, I open the back door like I was looking for something, closed the door and said, "oh it's on the front seat", his building was on the passenger side of the truck. I quickly went to the driver side where he couldn't see me, and opened the door, jumped in the truck, and started it up. As I did this, he ran around the driver side and let the dogs go, they were jumping up at the windows as I drove off in a hurry. When I got to another phone terminal, I called dispatch, and told them what happen and that the Cable Department needs to come out to the manhole to repair the problem, BUT whatever they do, do not go in his house, because there is a very angry man with DOGS.

On another day I received a repair order to go to ROXBURY MA. which is also a part of Boston. I normally work in the South End, Backbay, and Downtown area. Roxbury is a two-man area because of crime, and some telephone workers have been robbed. My next job was on Tremont Street near the South End boarder. The address was a three-story apartment building which was built in the 1930's. Tremont Street is a very long street and very busy. It used to be all cobblestone and with trolleys going up and down but that's all gone now. I arrived at the building and immediately went to the back of the house to check for her dial tone at the terminal in the backyard, and it wasn't there so the problem had to be in the house. I then went around front and rang the doorbell. I knew from the repair order, it was a woman over the intercom she asked, "who is it?" I told her who I was she said come on up I went up to the second floor and she open the door. She was a middle-aged African American woman with gray hair. She had a very pleasant personality. She asked if I would like some water or soda as she showed me where all the phone jacks were. I checked the kitchen phone where the wires were coming into the apartment from the terminal and the dial tone was there, so I told her I have to check the wires and each jack along the baseboard until I find the break. So, as I was crawling on the floor checking the wires in this long hallway, I heard a low growling and I looked to my right and down the hallway was a pit bull showing me his teeth.

I thought, "oh no not this again", but the lady was at the other end of the hallway and I was between the two. I started to get up really slowly because pit bulls are very quick, and down on my knees he would of went right for my throat. His growl. was getting louder. As I was getting up, I said to , in a very calm and quiet voice "Miss can you please put the dog away?" All of a sudden, she turned into the EXORCIST. She started screaming at me, " the dog lives here you don't, I'm not putting shit away". I started explaining to her, as I walked slowly to the door, there was no way I could fix her phone with that dog growling at me and he was coming down the hall slowly but he was still grrrrrr at me. As I got to the door, she said "you can't leave", and I said, "oh yeah?" I open the door and flew down the stairs when I got to the bottom she yelled out I'll put the dog away, I said to her, "it's too late, I am not going thru that again and you're going to be out of a telephone for a while because I am going to tell my dispatch what you refuse to do and they are not going to send another repair man out under these CIRCUMSTANCES". I was amazed at how quickly her personality changed, but this is just what we go through that's part of the job.

On another occasion, I called in and got a job from dispatch first thing in the morning, as I left the garage. I was feeling kind of tired. I am not really a morning person and some days are better than others. The repair order was for a three-story building in the South end of Boston it said to go to the landlord on the first floor to get the key to the customers room because she was at work. That's no problem, it happens all the time people have to work so they leave their apartment key with a neighbor. I got to the address; this was a rooming house. I rang the bell a voice said "hello". I replied, " telephone company" and the landlady open the door and said, "Ms. Jackson is expecting you". "Here's her key it's on the third-floor room #305". I took my tools and climbed up three flights. I had already gone to the back of the house through the alley and checked the phone terminal for dial tone, and it was there so I knew the problem most likely was in her room. I use the key and went in it was an efficiency apartment or some people call it a kitchenette, it had a large bed and a little sink and an area to do some cooking. The bathroom was outside the room, and down the hall which was shared by the other rooms on the same floor. I started checking the phone jacks that were along the floorboards on my knees. When I got to the jack that was by the bed, the jack was a little behind the bed post and I couldn't move the bed it was a waterbed so, I laid down on my stomach to reach around the bed post. At this point I just want to say, "I love animals", I had a pit bull for six years and I raised Akitas, my ex-wife and I were associated with the A.S.P.C.A and I am extremely against cruelty to animals.

But when you are surprised by something, in shock and scared all at the same time your reflex kicks in. All of a sudden, a Chihuahua came at me fast from under the bed growling and trying to bite my eyeball. It was a quarter of an inch from my eye coming from out of the dark. All I could see was its white teeth brushing my eye lid. In one motion, I jumped up and kicked, the dog. The dog hit the wall, fell on the bed, and ran off the bed to the other side of the room. When I saw those sharp teeth snapping at my eye, I almost pooped myself. I was still shaking, as I bent down and replaced that phone jack that looked like the dog had been chewing on. I didn't hear a peep out of the dog after he ran off the bed. He didn't know me, and was probably watching me the whole time I was in the room. He might have been scared and being protective, but he scared the mess out of me. I just hope he wasn't hurt too bad. I gathered up my tools, which went flying, and left. I shut the door and went downstairs, knocked on the land lady's door and handed her the keys and told her the phone is repaired. She said good, oh and by the way I forgot to tell you Ms. Jackson has a dog. I can hear him barking at night sometimes, did he get in the way? I said, "no, he must have been hiding, well have a good day", I said as I was leaving and thinking to myself, I could have used that information before I went up to the room.

WE CLIMB THE POLES IN ALL KIND OF WEATHER

Chapter 6
THE MACARBRE

In this world, we run across all kinds of strange things and even death. Here are a few of those. It was a typical morning at the telephone garage and I was getting my fist repair job from dispatch. They had told me that the customer had called in three times and his phone was still not fixed. I was also the fourth repair man to go out on this particular repair job. They said if the customer wasn't home, to go to the management office and they would let me in. This was an assistant living building in the Back Bay on St. Bothol Street. It was a brick building with five floors, kind of a nursing home, but the residence can come and go as they please and they have their own apartments. I first went to the back of the building to the phone terminal to check for the customers dial tone and it was there, so I went around to the front of the building and my repair order said Baker # 32. I rang the bell and got no answer, then I rang the management bell and they let me in. got to the office and a lady said, "I don't know if he is home right now but he has been complaining for over a week about his phone not working", well I rang the bell and there was no answer I told her, so she said, "Mr. Baker is in Apt. 32#, go on up there and I'll get a hold of the maintenance man and he'll meet you there".

I took the elevator to the third floor and knocked on Mr. Bakers door twice while I waited for maintenance. After about seven or eight minutes, the elevator door open and the maintenance man was hurrying towards me fumbling with a bunch of keys saying, " I am so glad you're here Mr. Baker has been a pain in the ass asking me how come his phone not fixed". Then I said, "l know the problem is in the building, and it could be in his apartment, but I won't know until I get inside". Well, he opens the door, and went in calling "Mr. Baker are you home?" I was inside standing by the door as he went searching through the apartment.

When he opened the door, I smelled something, and it got stronger as I stood there. I knew what it was it was the smell of death, and I was not going a step more into that room All of a sudden, the maintenance man, a gray-haired man in his 50's, came running full speed like Jesse Owens out of the bedroom yelling "he's dead! he's dead!" and shoved me out of his way up against the wall, heading for the elevator which was about thirty feet away. I was right behind him; he wasn't leaving me there with a dead guy. The smell was all in the hallway he must have been dead for over a week. The maintenance man told me that for weeks he was complaining about his phone, he said "l guess the phone company came out ranged his bell and when there was no answer they left, but I did notice that I haven't seen him for a while". I said, "yeah this is the reason you haven't seen him he's gone". Because the job was never closed out in the computer, for some reason dispatch kept sending people out to repair the problem, but this is one that can't be fixed.

On a nice spring day, I was dispatched a repair job to go to the wealthy part of the Back Bay of Boston, Massachusetts where people were financially in good shape. On Commonwealth Ave., there are some historic buildings, some houses had four floors some even had elevators in the house. When I arrived at the address, I went right to the phone terminal at the rear of the house to see if the customers dial tone was there and it was. So, I went to the front door and rang the bell. A little old lady answered the door she looked like a sweet old lady in her 80's close to 90. I told her I was there to fix her phone. She said, "come on in and would you like some refreshments?" I said no and she said, "well the phone down here in the kitchen works but the phone's upstairs in the bedrooms don't work". I checked the phone in the kitchen and got dial tone. As she took me over to the stairs, I could see that this was a large open space house with a lot of antique furniture that look like they dated back to the 1930's. There was a couple of cuckoo clocks that went off, she said "I'll meet you upstairs where my sister is I have to take the chair." The stairs were long, and curved. She sat down in one of those electric chairs that road on a rail up to the top, when she pushed the button and the chair took off. I thought the chair was going kind of fast because, in the movies they seemed to be going very slow. Well, I was walking and she beat me up the stairs, when I finally got up to the floor where the bedrooms where she introduces me to her sister who seem to be about the same age with more gray hair. They took me to their bedrooms at the end of the hall. As they did, we passed three other bedrooms with the doors shut. I didn't really pay much attention to those other rooms, I just wanted to get to the phones that didn't work. One of the sister's, her name was Blanche, took me to her room, it was at the very end of the hallway. She said, "my phone stopped working a few days ago". I check it and knew there was a break in the line from that phone to the kitchen phone, so I put my beeper on that phone jack and using my probe started tracing the sound from my beeper along the wire, that was going from room to room along the base board. The other sister, her name was Sue, showed me where her phone was in her room.

It was the same thing, no dial tone but I could hear my beeper loud and clear. So, I got to one of the doors that was closed and I told them "l have to get into this bedroom", they said "NO!" so I explain to them I have to get in there to see if the break in the line was in there they said NO again. Well, I said every time your phone rings you don't want to keep running down to the kitchen it's a long way from your bedroom. They finally said "okay", but as they open the door, one of the sisters ran into the room and was covering something up on one of the beds. As I said earlier, it was springtime 70 degrees outside and about 72 or 73 degrees in the house. When she opens that door, I felt cold air coming out that room like 40 degrees. When I stepped inside the room, it looked like a person in that bed that she was covering with a sheet. The other bed looked like a person partly covered, but I could see it and at first, I thought it was a store manikin. I went by both beds to the phone jack on the other side of the room and there was no dial tone there also. I kept my eye on those two beds. Well, it dawned on me that what I was looking at was TWO DEAD BODY'S! I don't know if these bodies were taken from a funeral home after they had been embalmed and brought back here and never buried, or they were mummified, and preserved for some cult reason. It was very cold in the room, and there was a strong odor, but it didn't smell like dead or rotten flesh, but I knew something was seriously wrong. These ladies were very old and maybe some how they found a way of keeping their dead relatives around. It looked like these corpses had been dead for years. I knew I had to get out of there. I went and took my buzzer off the other phone jack and told the ladies, “l needed some more tools out of my truck and I will be right back”. I went around back of the house to the phone terminal, and called my foreman and said to Bob you have got to see this!” When he came, I told him what I saw. We went into the house together, and I took him up to that room. The ladies were looking worried, but I knew this had to be done. We went into that bedroom, and he picked up one of the sheets and turned to me grabbed my arm, and said “we got to get out of here!” As we were running down the stairs, he said “WHAT THE HELL WAS THAT?” He told me “call dispatch, close this job out, and I am going back to my office and call the police, the board of health. and a funeral home!” I never knew what happen to the old ladies, but I know phone repair jobs don’t get much weirder than that.

Chapter 7

SEXUAL ENCOUNTERS

It seems like most of my memorable adventures as a telephone repair man happens towards the weekend. Monday, Tuesday and Wednesday are just your regular everyday common repair jobs and then Thursday, Friday, and Saturday, comes around and the stars and the zodiac are line up DIFFERENTLY. Dealing with the public, in their environment like I said before, when you ring the bell or knock on the door and say telephone company you never know who's going to answer the door. Over the years I have been approached by heterosexual women and homosexual men, here are a few instances. One Saturday morning, I came into work to do some over time I don't normally work on the weekend, but I thought I could use the money. I was out with some friends the night before partying so I wasn't 100% but I was very okay to do my job and I just wanted to get this day over with. My very first repair job was on Tremont Street in the South end of Boston, it was a Ms. Tucker on the repair order I got to the address and rang the bell. This was a basement apartment and she opened the door and said, "good your here, let me show you where the telephone box is". It's in the boiler room which was next to her apartment and I am thinking "good I don't have to climb a pole".

The lady was in her early thirties, very cute, average, build wearing a large tee shirt and no shoes. She went back to her apartment and I went into the boiler room. I checked and her dial tone was there at the box and I traced the wire back down the wall and it went into her place. I knocked on her door and she let me in complaining, "why is it always my phone I am sick of my phone not working?" Her room was a small kitchenette, with a bathroom, her bed took up much of the room. Across from the bed, was a nightstand with the phone on it, with a long cord. In the kitchen area was a small table. She told me the phone jack is under the nightstand. I picked the phone up and there was no dial tone, so I had to get down on my knees to take the jack apart. She sat on the bed straight across from me. She started telling me that she was a nurse and they thru her a going away party last night because she got promoted and was going to a new hospital. Then she said, "on the kitchen table there is some champagne in an ice bucket would you like some?" I said, "no I was out late myself and I just want to get your phone working". I took the jack off the wall and she had about a half of an inch of wire sticking out of the wall and the dial tone was there. Then she told me that she had moved the desk and the leg might have hit the jack. I had to get my long nose pliers and see if I could make a connection but I told her it wasn't going to be easy. As she sat across from me, I couldn't help noticing how short that tee shirt had gotten, and she was still complaining so I was trying to hurry up. Then she said, "I don't want to see you again but you know I always wanted to have sex with a utility man how about it?"

WHAT! I said, as I banged my head under the table. When I lifted my head up to hear what she said, and then she repeated it, I was startled and for a second, I thought am I on

Candid Camera? I was kind of shocked. It was so all of a sudden, but I manage to say okay. Well, she stood up lift her tee shirt up and took it off and she was buck naked, then she said, "I am going to jump in the shower so take your clothes off and have some champagne." I hurried up and fixed the jack and called dispatch and closed out the job, for a change they didn't put me on hold so it was done pretty quick. It was my first job of the day, so it was time for my break anyway. When she came out of the shower, I had my shoe's off, but that was all, I was still kind of leery. She said, "well get those pants off and get in bed." This was so hurried up that I didn't have time to get aroused, but she took care of that she started performing oral sex on me and I was ready. But before we start to have intercourse, she reached in her nightstand drawer that was on the other side of the bed, and took out a canister stuck it a little way in her vagina and sprayed it in like whipped cream. She said the medical name for it, and was some kind of germicide so she wouldn't get pregnant. Well, we didn't just have sex, I made love to her in different positions, and made her have six to eight orgasms. When we were through, she said "there is a clean towel on the sink so you can wash up." Before I left, she grabbed me, and gave me a long passionate kiss and said, "you have my number please call me so we can get together again." I said "really, you told me you didn't want to see me again." She said, "oh that was bull shit." She said, "the way you made me feel, I definitely want to see you again". I left, and what we did stayed on my mind for the next couple of repair jobs that day, but by the end of the day I had forgot all about it.

I just wanted to finish the day, turn in my work, and go home which I did. Now when I first became a telephone repairman, it was all paperwork. Years later, we got computers in the shape of a phone which we carried with us even up poles. I didn't think of Ms. Tucker until Sunday evening, and I realized I turned her phone number into my foreman with the rest of my work for that day. So, I couldn't wait to get to work Monday morning but my foreman said he already turned it in and it's in the database at Headquarters. Okay, I knew where she lived and over the next couple of weeks I went by a few times and rang the bell and got no answer. I remember she told me she was going to a new hospital and also moving very soon. Well, I will always remember that day, it was like two ships passing in the night. On a Thursday's a lot of the times, guys in the telephone garage would borrow money from each other. It was the day before payday, and some guys were broke from paying bills or just living from paycheck to paycheck. Now this didn't happen all the time but it happens, so they would get 10 or 20 so they could by lunch knowing they would get paid the next morning. I had got to my third repair job on Commonwealth Avenue, and I went around back of the house to check for dial tone at the rear wall terminal box and the dial tone was there so I knew the problem had to be in the house. I went around the front and rang the bell, a middle-aged Irish looking man with Grey hair open the door. He could see I. was from the phone company by all the tools I had draped over my shoulder. "Boy I am glad to see you my phones have been out for a few days", he said. "Well, I am here to help" I told him. He said he was hanging some Christmas lights up in the kitchen, and he though he nicked a wire going over the door frame with a hammer and nail. The door frame was tall so I told him I would need a latter to get up there to check, he said "l have a short step ladder, it's rickety, but it will hold you my roommate steadied me on it so I can help you". "Okay" I said. I had checked a connecting jack at the window seal where the wire was coming into the house from the outside. It was good there, so I had to trace the wire up over the door frame. As I got on the ladder, it was shaky and the customer grabbed my leg, and said "don't worry I got you". I saw that on top of the door frame there was a nail thru the wire. So, what I had to do was run a new wire from the window seal to the kitchen jack where he's wall phone was. Once I knew where the break in the wire was, it didn't take long to fix the problem.

The customer said, "thank you so very much can I get you anything?" I said "no, all I have to do now is call my dispatch and close out the job". He had gone around to all his phones and said there all good. Then he said, "you can use this phone here in the living room". There was a phone on a desk next to the couch which he sat down on. So, I am standing next to the phone, on hold, with dispatch. I was looking at my notes in my hand, and he was watching television. Then he said, "you ever seen adult movies? and I looked at the television, and it was a porno movie. It was two girls and a guy, I said "yeah, I have a few of them myself." At this point dispatch came back on the phone to tell me hold on for another couple of minutes and I said okay. As I looked back to the television, the screen had changed, it was a black man and two white guys on the television, one guy had the black guy's penis in his mouth and the other guy was licking his balls. I was standing between the couch and television, and I immediately turn to the couch. He had his dick out of his pants stroking it. He put twenty dollars on the desk, next to the couch, and said "let me suck you off I am really good at it". I thought oh boy here we go. It through me off for a second, because he didn't look like he was homosexual. So, I said to him in a nice way "thanks but no thanks, I am not gay". He was still jerking himself and said "that's okay. I can make you feel really good", as he put two more twenties on the table. Appealing as that sounded, looking at the sixty dollars on the table, and remembering I had borrowed twenty dollars that morning in the telephone garage, I told him "that was not going to happen", and I am still on hold with dispatch. All of a sudden, his roommate came in the house. He was a younger man with black hair maybe Italian. The customer on the couch said "Jamie, the phone man is here". Jamie from across the room, came towards me swishing, and I could tell this guy was gay and proud of it. He kept saying "the phone man is here; the phone man is here". In a high pitch voice Jaime said, "you guys didn't start partying without me, did you?" At that point, dispatch came back on the phone, which I still had up to my ear. I knew I had to get out of there so I told dispatch "the customer has to leave for work right now so I will close out the job from another location". I told the men that their phones were all set and have a good day. As I was leavening, the roommate said, "well come back some time and party with us". I said "yeah, okay", but I knew I wasn't doing that. It was just another day in the life of a telephone repairman.

Chapter 7a

SEXUAL ENCOUNTERS

It was a Saturday morning, and I was in the phone company garage, on one of the many phones there, getting my work from dispatch. They gave me three for the morning and said you might want to do the one on Boylston Street first, because there is supposed to be some kind of parade happening on that street sometime today. Well, it was up to me to decide which one to do, and in what order, since there wasn't a customer saying we had better be there at a certain time, and of the repair jobs were closer to the garage. It was a nice seasonal day around 75 degrees, and I went and did Ovo of the jobs. I then when on break and went on Boylston Street.

This was a pay phone job down in a subway across from the Coply Boston Public Library and a bout twenty yards from where the Boston Marathon finish line was. It was a busy street as usual, and I parked the phone truck right in front of the Coply subway station. I went down the stairs into the subway. I had my tools with me, and I went over to the token booth and asked the man in the booth "which payphone was out of order?" and he said, "all the way down the platform, it's the first phone you get to". I got to the phone and took it apart and found that the phone was okay, but there was no dial tone coming from the terminal which was located behind one of the four locked doors on the platform.

So, I had to go ask the guy in the token booth which door was the phone terminal in and did he have the key, "he said no but he'll call the head security guy to open it for me". Well as I was waiting the subway trains kept pulling up and more and more people were getting off much more than usually would be for a Saturday morning. Then I noticed the people were starting to be wearing costumes of all kinds.

As I stood there, more and more people with costumes of all different colors filled the platform and it was packed, as they all went upstairs to Boylston street. I went back to the guy in the token booth and asked him "hey, when is that guy coming with the key? I have been waiting for over thirty minutes? he then said, "he is on his way but he had an emergency at another subway". So, I went and sat back down watching the people getting off the trains with all these strange costumes.

Finally, the man came with the key, and he says, "I got held up getting here with all the commotion up on the streets". Well, I didn't really pay much attention to what he was saying, because I just wanted to get into the phone terminal room get the dial tone to the payphone and leave. As I got to the terminal, I realize the dial tone wasn't coming from the CO. (Central Office). On the terminal itself, there is fifty binding post which is in pairs a tip and ring. The dial tone comes from the CO. On one side tip and goes back on the other side the ring which completes the circuit. Ten of the binding post went to the payphones on the platform and one went to the token booth. So, I get my ohm meter out to test a spare pair going back to the CO, and then change the wiring at the terminal, and the guy at the CO. will change it at his end. We'll all this takes time, when I finished, I told the guy in the booth the payphone is all set and went back up the stairs to my truck. When I got to the street I WAS IN SHOCK, the city had removed all the cars on the street except my phone truck and there was a parade going on like I had never seen before. There were giant floats with men half naked going by some in very colorful costumes. Some with just a thong on and then there were other floats with women with costumes and some with thongs and pasties on. There were floats with men and women dancing and some were humping each other.

The music was very loud and the sidewalk was packed right into the street. This was a big, big, party going on, and I was stuck right in the middle of the first GAY PRIDE PARADE, that I was aware of here in Boston. I had other repair jobs to get to, but I wasn't going anywhere. I was surrounded by people that were dancing on the sidewalk, and all in the streets between the floats. I had to admit it this was quite the spectacle. I went back down into the subway and called my dispatch and told them what was happening. I had also told dispatch that had no idea when it was over, they said there was nothing I could do, so just enjoy the show. So, I went back up and watched the parade. As I am standing there observing the parade, a man and his wife I knew from the neighborhood walked up to me and jokingly said "so are you apart of this?" I said back to him "now you see the phone truck parked here", then he said, "I was only kidding". His wife said, "hey you guys check that out", as we turned him and I saw about fifteen feet away a group of women on a side street dancing, all colors, ages, shapes and sizes with no tops on. Well, my friend and his wife continued down Boylston street but I stayed until it was over and when it was my day was done, not being gay, what an experience, watching all this. I know there has been many gay pride parades all over the country since then, but that was the first that I ever knew of and I'll never forget.

Chapter 8

DANGER, MUGGERS

In Boston, is where I started with the phone company. I lived a little under Wo miles away from the telephone garage in the South End. It was a very diverse group of people, a mixture of Puerto Rican, Chinese, Black, and White, in one community, in the South End, and everybody got along great. The Mayor would have free concerts in

Black Stone Park. Everybody would be there having a good time. Every now and then, I would jog to work from my apartment down Shawmut Avenue, to the phone company garage, just to try and stay in shape.

One Saturday morning, around six o'clock, I was jogging down the middle of the street, which I did just in case a dog darted out between a parked car, and try to bite me. There wasn't any leash law in Boston at that time, and dogs and wild cats were seen a lot. As I was jogging, I heard a woman screaming.

I couldn't tell at first where it was coming from because the street was lined up with park cars on both sides of the street. Then I saw about forty yards away, a black man with his arm around a Chinese woman's neck, trying to pull her into a doorway. She had a shopping bag in both hands, and her keys in her other hand. Apparently, she lived there and he must had sneaked up on her and jumped her as she opened the door.

I sped up and yelled "let her go!" this guy looked like he was in his Twenties, and at that time I was in my mid-thirties. He started back peddling dropping her, and reaching for something in his back pocket. But it was too late, I was on him and I hit him with a left jab, and he went down. He scuffled to his feet, still looking for something in his back pocket. Whatever it was, he didn't have it, so he took off down a side street. If I had hit him with my right fist, he would have been out cold. I stood there for about a minute, watching the lady in her fifties, picking up her bags and saying something in Chinese to me. I was saying to her and motioning for her to get in the building, because I was a little worried that he might come back. Once she was in and the door was locked, I started jogging again, thinking what might had happen if I had not have come along?

She had been shopping, so he most likely was going to rob her, or might even raped and killed her once he got her inside that building. When I got to the garage, I told the other repair men what had happen. They were all amazed, and said "it's a good thing you were there you probably saved her life". Then one of the guys said, "you know in some Asian customs if you save someone's life, they owe you their life forever they become your slave". I said, "there's been enough of that in this country and around the world, I was just glad I was able to help her"

On another occasion it was a Wednesday and towards the end of the day, I was feeling tired, and I had a repair job in the South End at the Cathedral Projects. This project was next to the Cathedral Church on one side, and Black Stone Park on the other side. The bad side where they have been a lot of muggings, a couple of the men worked with got mugged sitting in their truck at lunch time. So, some of the guys got a little nervous going into the project to repair phones.

There were tons of good people that lived there, but like a lot of projects, there are also a few bad apples. Underneath one of the buildings in the middle of the project, was a basement where a large room containing the phone and electrical terminals were. I always check there first to see if the customers dial tone was coming into the project, and it was so I headed to the customers apartment. When I got to the building, my work order read Lopez apartment 5W. I knew it was going to be a climb, because the elevators never seem to work and they always smell like pee and the intercom didn't work. As I am going up the stairs on the third floor, I passed these two guys and I said "hi". They replied and said hi, and I kept going to the fifth floor. When I got to the customers apartment, I was about six feet away from the door, and I saw those two guys coming up behind me.

Right away, I knew what they wanted to do, ROB me. The door was at the end of the hallway, and it was very narrow, about five feet wide, and I was boxed in. They were about eight feet away, but moving slowly towards me. They looked like they were in their twenties, and at the time I was in my late thirties. Back then, muggers and thugs didn't all carried guns, but I was pretty sure they had knives even though they hadn't pulled them out yet. All I had to defend myself, was my tool belt which was around my shoulder. In the belt, was a couple of screw drivers in different sizes. One was about fourteen inches long, so I pulled it out where they didn't see it by my side. I knew if the customer wasn't home, I would be fighting for my life, and I had no room to move around.

It was two against one, and I was cornered, but the warrior in me knew I was about to start swinging and kicking like crazy. I hurried to the door and banged on it hard (normally I would have knocked like somebody with some sense but I was desperate). GOD was with me, Miss Lopez opens the door, and those guys ran up about five feet from me when I pushed my way into her apartment. I shut the door behind me as I said, "telephone company". I apologized to her, and told her what was about to happen in the hallway if she hadn't opened the door. She then said, "there have been a lot of robberies a round here and were trying to move". She had a very decorative apartment in a Puerto Rican style, which was very nice. She took me over to her kitchen wall phone, which is usually the first place the dial tone comes into the apartment. I took the phone off the wall, and about thirty roaches crawled out the wall jack from inside the wall. I knew that was the problem, so I took her broom and brushed them away hung the phone back up and there was dial tone. The roaches had cluttered together and short circuited the line. She knew she had roaches, but she didn't know they could do that. Miss Lopez was very grateful that I fixed her phone, and I was grateful she was home. As I left her apartment, I peeked out the door, to see if those thugs were still out there. They were gone, so I ran down five flights as fast as I can to get to the outside. I was still angry at those guys for putting me in that situation, so when I got to the phone truck, I put my tools away and took out my hammer and was going to go thru the project looking for them. Outside I had plenty of room to move around "its hammer time! but then I thought that God made away for me to get through this without getting hurt. I always told my son trouble is easy to get into and hard to get out. So, I put the hammer back in the truck and left, but that was very scary being cornered like that in the hallway.

Chapter 9
THE MORGUE

I was in the phone company garage one morning running late, I was almost always running late I guess I am not a morning guy, but I am always on time. I had got a repair order to go the City of Boston on Massachusetts Avenue. The number on the repair order was a very low number, and I have been up and down Mass Avenue a thousand times. So, I just knew it had to be at the Boston City Hospital, which over the years, I have been there for one thing or another, from a broken arm to a tooth being pulled, and whenever I was really sick. So, I pulled up in the parking lot and grabbed my tools. I went in and up to the front desk and said, " telephone company, I am here to fix the phone that's out of order".

The lady at the front desk looked at the address and said, "oh you want the building across the street, it's the Morgue". Oh wow, the morgue! I turned around and went to that building she pointed to. I have seen that building many times driving by but never really paid much attention to it. It was a drab looking building, and I never saw anyone going in there, were as the hospital was always buzzing all day long. I parked got my tools and went inside, it was a large building so, I asked someone going by where the office was. When I got to the office, they showed me that they had a multi-complex system, and one of the lines was out.

The building must have had over thirty different phone lines. I told the guy in the office that I have to get to the phone terminal and according to my repair order, it's in the basement. "Can anybody show me where it's at?" I said and he replied, "sure I'll show you". I followed him down the corridor until we got to these big doors. When he opened the doors, he said "we have to through here to get to the stairs leading to the basement." It was a large room, with what looked like giant file cabinets, one on top of another. They were arranged from the floor to the high ceiling in the walls all around the room, and it was very cold in there. I stopped for a second, looked around the room.

A chill came over me, not everybody in their everyday life finds themselves surrounded by dead bodies. So, I said "okay let's get to that terminal." I followed him through a door which was on the other side of the room and down the stairs to the basement. He showed me where the phone terminal was and then he said, "do you know how to get back to the office?" I said, "yes the way we came down", and then he went back. After I examined the terminal, I had to go back to the office through the dead room and I felt eerie, so I scurried thru the room and got back to the office. Checking the phone lines in the office, I found that I had to go back to the basement one more time. Now I am no scaredy cat, but I knew I had to go back through that room even though I didn't want to. When I got to that room and open up those double doors there it was, a hospital gurney with a dead body.

It was partly covered with a bloody sheet, up to the top of the man's head. Part of his head was missing, and there was blood and brain matter dripping down from the gurney to the floor, it was thick and gooey looking. My jaw dropped, and a chill came over me. I have never seen anything like this before. The guy must have just been killed, and they rushed him over to the morgue, and left him here in the middle of the room just where I had to pass to get to that door leading to the basement. I just wanted to finish this job, so I ran by the dead body not looking at him got to the basement. At the phone terminal I was able to put that phone line back in service. The guy who showed me where the terminal was his name was Jim. So, I went on another line and called the phone number that was out and Jim answered the phone I said, "your all set" and he said, "thank you". I told him what I saw and he said, "oh yeah, when somebody is just killed the ambulance people will bring them in here and leave the body for us to put them away." Well, I asked Jim was there another way out of the basement because I do not want to go through that room again. He laughed , and said "sure at the other end of the basement, you'll see another door you can go out that way." "I just took you the short way but the other door takes you the length of the building" I told him "thank you, I am taking the long way out." When I got back to the phone truck, I just sat there for a minute. I just couldn't get that image out of my head, and after all these years I still can't.

SOME DAYS WERE BETTER THAN OTHERS

Chapter 10
MENTAL CAMPUS

I was assigned to repair a payphone on a nice spring afternoon, at a large college campus. It was a facility between Belmont and Arlington Massachusetts, which was the mentally impaired. To get there I had to travel down the longest street in the state, Massachusetts Avenue. It starts at lower Dorchester Avenue, and bordering on south Boston, which was through the South End to the Back Bay, and into Cambridge through to Arlington and Belmont Massachusetts. When I got there, I saw it was a big area with a lot of different housing with plenty of space between them. Each housing was for a different age group. It was a rehabilitation or treatment facility.

There was one for adolescents, another for upper teens and twenties, and another for middle age, and then seniors and elderly. I had been there several times repairing different payphones in different building, but the very first time there it was quite an experience. It was at the young people's place building number two. I had to search around the campus, it was like a golf course with houses on it. I pulled up to the front door, got my tools and rang the bell. I notice there were some construction trucks parked on the side of the building, but I really didn't pay much attention to them. A man slid open a slot on a big iron door, and said "who is it?" I said, "telephone company, do you have a payphone out of order?" He said, "oh yes, come on in".

As he opens the door, he said "follow me, I'll show you where it is." He said, "I have no idea what these kids did to the phone this time." We went down this long hallway, and as we were walking, I notice there was a young couple in their teens or twenties making out against the wall. The guy said, "pay no attention to them, you'll see a lot of different things here." There were some kids spray painting graffiti on the walls, some kids were just standing there screaming as loud as they can, and there were people chasing each other and throwing stuff at each other. When we got to the pay phone, I said "wow, quite a place!" and he said, "yes these are trouble kids with mental problems, and that nobody cares for anymore, and we are trying to help," I said, "bless you, we need more people like you and your coworkers in this world to help other people." Now back then, we didn't have cell phones but he had a walkie talkie on his hip. I heard loud and clear "Jason, we need you in the containment room!" He turned to me and said, "I have an emergency, I'll be back." Well, I fixed the problem. Someone had pried the phone off the wall, just enough to cut the wire, and then put the phone back, so you couldn't tell what was wrong. I looked around for Jason, and I couldn't find him, but I knew where the door was.

As I was walking down the hallway, I asked a couple of people "excuse me do you know where Jason is?" they just ignored me. I saw that couple that was making out, and now they're on the floor feeling all over each other. I got to the door, and it was locked. All of Jason's coworkers were probably helping him wherever he was at. Then, I saw a girl, coming towards, me really slow, and I said, " excuse me, do you know how I could get out this door?" She looked like she was in a trance, zombie like. She walked about a foot away from me and kept walking passed me. She then slammed into the iron door face first. She turned around, and started walking back .to me. Blood was coming out of her nose. She was blonde, skinny, girl about twenty years old. Now she really looked like a zombie! I stepped out of her way as she kept walking back down the hallway. I said "shit, I have got to get out of here!"

There was another door to a room, next to the main door, I heard construction going on in there. I don't know if they were remodeling or adding on the building, but I needed to get out. So, I tried the doorknob, and it was locked. I could hear drilling and hammering in there, so I started banging on the door. At first there was no response. I kept banging on the door, and the construction stopped. Then the door slowly cracked open, and a guy peeked out, with one eye, and said "may I help you?" I said "yes, I am with the phone company, and I was working on the payphone." "The guy who let me in here disappeared!" Sure, he said, "there was another guy knocking on the door, and said he was GEORGE WASHINGTON, and he was looking for his army!" "Whoa", I said "go look outside your window in there or your door, you will see a phone truck." He closed the door, and I could hear him say to the other guys, "it's some guy in there claiming he's with the phone company and got locked in there by mistake", then I heard someone else say "yeah sure he is!" It was like they didn't believe me! So, I am standing there shaking my head, and thinking what the Heck!" Then the door opens wide, and the guy said, "get in here quick!" and slam the door shut and locked it. Well, you can't be too careful, and we have been here about two weeks putting on an extension. We have heard all kinds of sounds in there, and people knocking saying they are different famous people. I thanked the guys, and left. As I was driving away, I was thinking this a private funding facility, in a small town, and it was good that the town had the money to help those kids get the treatment, and medicine they needed.

Chapter 11

COIN COLLECTOR:

In the telephone company, at the time, before my retirement, I worked in many different departments. One of them was part of the Payphone Department., which was the coin collection, which I did for a while. Of all the jobs, I did in the phone company, this was the hardest. The actual collecting of the coins out of the payphones was easy, it was getting to all the payphones in one day, that was the hard part. To get the money out of the phone, I had a key which I put in the face plate on the bottom of the payphone. You had to turn the key and take off the plate, reach in and pull the full money box out, put and put it in a case which held four boxes. You had to put in an empty box, and then lock it back up. When there are four full boxes in the case, I would take the case back to the phone truck which had a carousel that would turn around and I would put each box in the carousel and lock it. Each payphone had its own number, and when the phone gets backed up with coins, the payphone will not work. Somebody will call it in or they can tell from the Coin Office, that a certain payphone is out of order. It literally only takes seconds to change the box.

In the morning, were given a lot of stops for the day to make up for the eight hours in your shift. Each payphone is one stop, and sometimes we would get sixty to eighty stops. Back then, we didn't have GPS, we had a big Atlas street map book, which we had to find payphones in different cities in Massachusetts. Once I find the city, then I had to find the address of the building. It could be a factory with four payphones, and I am there sometimes to collect only one I have to go to different floors and ask around to find that one. But a lot of times dispatch will wait until there are a few phones in the same area that was out of order. Then they would send me out to collect from those phones. Now days,

I can't remember the last time I saw a payphone, but for years and years people used payphone. I think ninety eight percent of those people had never seen a coin collector. We were like "the men in black", as if you're talking on a payphone there's a payphone next to you, and a person is there, you turn around and they are gone, and that's how quick the coin collectors collect the coins out of the payphones, especially outside or in a subway station or airport. The exception is at a bar where sometimes when you pulled the coin box out, there is an overflow of coins, and nickels, dimes and quarters are all over the floor, and people rushed over to pick up the coins, saying they lost money in the payphones. Before I leave the garage, after got my order of stops for the day, I would go to the guard shack to get a security guard to ride with me for safety. If I am in Boston that day, I did need a security guard, but if I was going to be in the suburbs, I didn't need one.

One morning I got my collection orders for the day, and one stop was for Deer Island in East Boston. I had never been there, but I've heard about it, and it was a prison. I had a security guard with me at the time, and when I got to the prison, the guard said, "if you want, I can wait here and guard the carousel because the prison guards inside can take you where you need to go." "I said okay" and got my empty case of coin boxes and went inside. I had to go through three different doors, and be searched from head to toe, even though the prison guards knew I was with the phone company to collect from the payphones. I had to chuckle to myself, that it almost seems as hard to get in the prison as it is to break out. One of the guards took me through the prison, and I noticed the prison cells and the inmates watching me wondering what I was doing there with this case in my hand. We got to the phone room and there were inmates in there using some of the phones. There were eight phones, and two of them were out of order. As I was walking with the security guard, I notice he didn't have a gun on him. I asked him about it, and he said, "for safety", they're not allowed to wear the gun around inmates because of the fear that they could easily grab the gun. I thought from watching movies they always carried them. Well, we were in the payphone room, and I started to take one of the full coin boxes out of the phone, when some coins started falling on the floor. The inmates started reaching for the coins. I normally would pick them up, and put the coins in an overflow bag, which we carried, but these guys jumped down on the floor and were grabbing the coins. The prison guard said to them, " back off and give those coins to the phone man" which they did. However, at the same time, they were saying they lost money in those phones, just like people do at a bar. When that happens, I usually tell them to call the phone company and tell them how much they lost, and the phone company will reimburse them. I don't know exactly how that would work in a prison, but I know that I didn't have the authority to give people coins back. The prison guard turned to me and said "I'll be right back: he had got a call on his walkie talkie. "Whoa!" I whispered to him, "you can't leave me in this locked room with these prisoners!" His response was (and I'll never forget it) "what are they going to do to you they're already in prison!" I don't know if this guy thought he was a comedian, but to me, that wasn't funny. Then he left and the door locked behind him. Immediately the prisoners started gathering around, asking me to give them some money, even the guys that were on the phones stopped talking and came over. There were coins all over the floor from me pulling the full box out and these coins were jammed up in the housing of the phone. I had started picking them up, but I stood up when they got closer. Just then the door opened, and the prison guard came in. The prisoners all moved back . He asked me, "is everything alright?" I said "yeah, I just want to finish up and get out of here". I picked up the coins, and put them in the overflow bag, changed the boxes, and asked him to show me the way out. When I got to the coin truck, I said to the security guard, " if I ever collect from a payphone in a prison again, you're coming in with me", he laughed and said, "why did they try to rob you?" I just looked at him and said, "almost", as we drove off.

Chapter 12

THE COIN COLLECTOR

As a coin collector, one of the things the phone company was worried about was people stealing. One of the ways managements would watch for theft, was to treat a dime with a certain chemical, and put it in a random payphone. When that payphone was collected, they would look for that dime using a special magnifying glass. If they couldn't find that one dime out of over two hundred coins that came out of that one box, you could be suspended or fired for stealing. Even if that dime rolled under a heavy obstacle, like a refrigerator that I can't move, I could be in trouble because they want to see THAT dime and even if you replaced it with your own dime, it wouldn't matter. Now they didn't do that all the time, just randomly to keep people honest.

One day I couldn't wait to get off work and go home. I know some days are harder than others and this was a hard one. You know how some days, it seemed like everything was going wrong. Well, I had finally got back to the garage, unloaded the carousel, and put the phone truck away. I was finally able to get in my car and go home. I was relaxing on the couch watching television, and the news was on. I wasn't really paying attention, I still thinking about the bad day I had and was glad I am home. The news started showing Logan Airport and all that five o'clock traffic that's always there at that time. They started showing footage at the payphones at the airport. The airport has the most stop's, they're all in one place, but on different floors with a hundred and twenty phones all over the place which is quite a lot. The camera started zooming in on a group of ten payphones with that yellow crime scene tape roped off. About ten feet from the pay phones with the yellow crime scene tape all around them. One of the Airport Police was directing everybody stay back. People were gathered around the tape wondering what's going on. I am home watching this wondering myself what is this about. The cop was about ten feet away from the payphones, with his hands up at the crowd still saying backed up, and telling everybody the Bomb Squad is on its way here. The camera zoomed in to the top of one of the payphones, and there it, was a black coin box. The news camera zoomed back out to show the crowd. All of a sudden, I saw East, a guy who also works as a coin collector, run through the crowd and jump over the yellow tape. He ran around the police officer saying, "excuse me" and he ran up to the payphone and grabbed the box. When he did that, the officer yelled "everybody down!" The officer hit the ground and people started running and falling down. East just ran jumped over the yellow tape and took off through the crowd. He went back to his phone truck which was parked outside. Well, I fell off the couch laughing, I almost pissed my pants. WOW that was LOL situation. It was hysterical! I even called a few people to see if they were watching the news at that moment.

Nobody at the airport knew what that little black box was, so they just assumed it was a bomb. It was just a mistake on East's part. I don't know if he was tired that day, but when you have to collect coins from a hundred and twenty payphone's things can happen. It started when he originally got back to the garage to close out for the day. When they took the carousel off the coin truck and counted the boxes, they found that one box was missing. That was the moment that East realized what had happened. Being in a hurry and trying to beat that long rush hour traffic and the airport traffic, he had mistakenly put the full box on top of the phone, and the empty box into the payphone locked it up and left. Even though he went back to the airport through all that traffic again and retrieved it he got suspended. He was gone for a while and then he transferred into the Installation Department. I didn't see him for almost a year after that, but when I did see him, I started laughing all over again because that was a funny mess.

Chapter 13

THE FEUD

It was midday, and I was headed to my next repair job which was in the South End of Boston not too far from the telephone company garage. It was another rooming house with four floors and front and back apartments. I pulled up to the address and grabbed all of my tools, and decided to walk around the back of the building to the rear wall terminal. I checked for dial tone, and the customer's dial tone was there. I looked at the drop line going into the building and it was fine no breaks and it was going into the back window on the first floor. I went around to the front and rang the bell. A senior gentleman opened the door , and I said, "hi Mr. Brown, I'm with the phone company and here to fix your phone." "Come on in" he said, "my apartment is right here, as he was pointing at the front apartment on the first floor. It was small in square footage, with a lot of antiques and military stuff. He happened to be wearing a Vietnam Veteran hat. He was really upset about his phone being off, but I am used to that angry, customers , about 60 % are. So, I try to calm them down, but this was a little different . Mr. Brown knew what the cause of his phone not working was. So, he started yelling "he did it again! he did it again." I asked, "what are you talking about?" Mr. Brown replied, "my asshole neighbor! he cut my phone line again!" "WHAT!" I said "He cut your line? Who did this?" I asked. Mr. Brown told me it was the guy in the back apartment. So, I put my beeper on his phone jack after I checked it for dial tone and started tracing the wires down the hallway towards the back apartment.

When I arrived at the door, the customer was right behind me yelling "you're in trouble now the phone company is here!" I told him "listen, you go back to your room while I talk to this guy." I knocked on the door, and another gray haired senior open the door, and said "what do you want?" I said, "I am with the phone company, and I have to check the phone." I told him "if I can't get to the wires coming in at the back window ,the whole building could be out of service", of course this wasn't true because each floor had its own entrance, but I knew I had to get into that window. So, he let me in and as I approached the window I saw the problem, he had taken a screwdriver and disconnected the box at the window, the wires going to the front apartment was sticking all out. Apparently, he had done this before, I connected the wires back and turn to him and I knew whatever I told him had to be good, so he wouldn't do this again. I said, "look you cannot do this it's a federal offense! you are violating an F.C.C. Regulation, and they already know you have done this before, and that was your first offense and this is your second, one more time and you're going to be arrested and go to prison for two years mandatory." His response was, "but I hate that guy." I told him "you're going to have to find some way to get along, or do you want to go to jail?" "He said no I won't do it again". He didn't close the door all the way, when he let me in, because we heard yelling from his front room and he was saying "he cut my wires again!" It was the customer from the front apartment had come partly into this guy's room. The guy I was talking to ran out to meet him screaming, "get out of my room!" I jumped between them like a referee in a boxing match. These two elderly gray-haired men in their late seventy's or early eighty's going at each other yelling was kind of funny until the customer in the front apartment said, "if you cut my phone line again, I'll blow your head off' and the other one said, "oh yeah, I'll get my gun right now". "WHOA!" I said. I actually grabbed both guys by the arm, and said "look the phone line is fixed, and he's not going to bother with your line again". I looked at the guy and "said right?' He said "yes". I then looked at my customer and said, "you can't keep threatening your neighbor or you will get arrested, do you understand?" He said "yes" I went on to say, "when you guys see each other in the hallway don't even speak just keep moving on that way no one gets hurt and no one goes to jail, because the law enforcement are aware of what's going on in this building and the police will be watching."

As a coincidence, in the South End of Boston Police Station Number Four was only a hundred yards away on the same street and they knew that. I checked the customers phone, and it was on but, before I left, I asked them both "are you guys going to be alright?" and they said "yes, okay I said no more Hatfield's and McCoy's I" I gathered up my tools, and got into my truck, and I thought it was good being a peacemaker for a change.

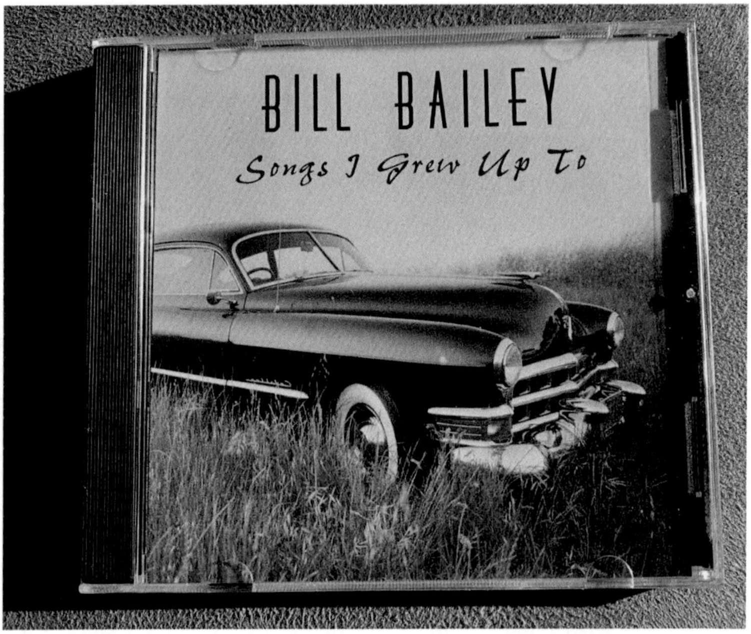

MY CD SOLD AROUND THE WORLD

Chapter 14

YWCA

While I was in the Payphone Department, I had a couple of repair jobs at facilities concerning women. Some of the places were for abused and battered women. One facility was in the South End of Boston at Rosie's Place, on Washington Street. It was a nice summer day, when I got a repair job from dispatch to go to Rosie's Place. I knew where it was, because it's on a major street and we pass it every day going back and forth to work. The building is considered a brown stone with four floors. The office was on the basement floor. I pulled the telephone truck in front, and rang the bell once, and there was no answer. Instead of ringing the bell again, I thought I would go around back to the rear wall terminal, and check for dial tone there since I knew I didn't have to climb a pole. I counted the number of houses out front, so when I went in the back alley, I would know which building it was, just in case there weren't any numbers back there. I open a little small gate, and walked thru a little yard to the terminal on the wall. Opening the box, I saw that the dial tone was there on the right binding post, so that was good. The back door was open, and through the screen door I could see the payphone in the basement on the wall. I pulled on the screen door, and it was not locked. The payphone was about twenty-five feet away, and I knew if I could get to the phone I would know if it's the phone, that's out of order by the phone number. I stepped in the basement all the while saying, "hello, hello, hello, telephone company!" Well, there was nobody around, so I went over to the phone and looked at the number, it matched my repair order and there was no dial tone.

Now this basement had some doors on the other side of the hallway wall with offices in them, and all of a sudden, a door flew open at the end of the hall and this woman came running at me at full speed. She was much bigger than me around six feet and two hundred forty pounds, saying " what the f---k are you doing in here,". She startled me the way she came at me, if it was a man, I might have drop kick him off of me, but because it was a woman, I didn't want to hurt her. She ran up and grabbed me by the arm yelling "man on the floor, man on the floor", as she was shaking me. At the same time, I am trying to explain who I am, and what I was doing there. I thru my hands in the air, and said "please calm down, I am with the phone company you can see all these tools on me and I am just here to fix this phone, it is out of order, right?" She stopped yelling, and said "yes, we been trying to get the phone company out here for almost a week," I said, "yeah we been back logged for a while, but am here now to put you back in service", then she said, "why didn't you ring the bell out front?" told her "I did but nobody came, so I went around back to check your line at the terminal then I saw the phone here in the hallway". Her AITITUDE really changed as we started talking, she said "so do you think you can fix it, oh yes this will be no problem." Then she told me "we had a break in and a couple of women's ex-boyfriends and or husbands had tried to get in and kill them over the years we have been here so we can't be too careful, the women that stay here a lot of them are afraid of men". I told her that I understand completely and was glad to help. She shook my hand and said, "thank you". I left, but next time I am going to keep banging on the front door until someone answers before I go around and into the back door!

Another repair job I had one day was on Berkeley Street at the Y.W.C.A., which was between the South End and the Back Bay of Boston. It was in the early morning of a nice summer day, and I pulled up to the front door, got my tools, and went inside to the front desk . There was a lady at the front desk and I said "hi, telephone company. Do you have a payphone out of order?", she said "yes, its upstairs, but you're going to have to wait until the security guard comes in and she will take you up to the phone". I asked the lady at the desk, did she know where the utility room was and she said "yes, take the elevator down to the basement, take a right, go down the hall and you will see the room". When I got to the phone terminal, I saw that the dial tone was there, so I knew had to get to the phone to fix it. I went back upstairs to the front desk, and told the lady that everything is fine at the phone terminal, and

I just got to get to the phone. She said to me "the security guard hasn't come in yet, and we don't usually let people upstairs if you don't live here unless accompanied by security. But go ahead it's on the third floor, just down from the elevator", I said "thank you this shouldn't take long". When I got to the payphone, and started taking the housing off the phone, a woman came out her room and started screaming "Man on the floor, Man on the floor", and ran back into her room. I was like are you kidding me oh no not again? So, I yelled back towards her room, " I am with the telephone company, I am just here to fix the payphone". Other people stuck their heads out to see what the commotion was all about. One lady said pointing to the room of the lady, was that her that was yelling? I said "yes. She said, "pay her no mind, she's crazy she is always yelling about something am just glad you're here to fix that payphone Mr. phone man". I said "thanks" and continued on and repaired the phone. When I got back down to the front desk, I told the lady, the phones all set. She said, "that's good that it's done, because the security called and said she'll be late, and oh by the way as she giggled, did the woman in 303 come out and yell at you?" "Yes, she did! I told her". She said I am sorry; I should have warned you about her. I said, "oh that's okay, it was not a problem". I told her "the phone is repaired and everything is good and have a nice day".

Chapter 15

THAT SMELL

Back in the day, in downtown Boston Massachusetts, when I was in my twenties, that area was called the Combat Zone. There were a lot of crimes being committed. It was also well known as the Red-Light District, with people getting robbed and prostitutes were everywhere. At that time, the law down there was known as the Tactical Police Force.

Those police officers were huge, and very big. Most of the police officers there weighted over three hundred pounds. There were clubs we use to go to and see entertainment. To my friends and I, in our early twenties, it was a very exciting time. We would see recording stars, and different groups that came to town. But then it all started to change, the entertainment clubs became strip bars, and X-rated movie houses also some bars, turned into booths where people did all kind of sexual things. Being young, this was all new to us. We sometimes would on the weekends' go downtown just to check out the ladies. No matter where you go down there, you could smell the smell of sex everywhere. At that time, we were curious and impressionable but after a while that area became old hat. The newness wore off, and we stopped going down there, but I never forgot that smell.

That area of downtown now has expanded into Chinatown it's all restaurants and stores and businesses. Oh boy! how things have changed for the better over the years. Later on, in this segment of my encounters on being a telephone repairman, I will let you know why I brought up the things that went on in downtown Boston, better known as the Combat Zone, back then. That was all before I started working for the telephone company. Some years later, after being a repairman I got a repair order to go to the Brookline, Massachusetts boarder on Commonwealth Avenue, it was a Saturday afternoon on a nice summer day. This telephone repair order was a Catholic Cathedral with acres and acres of land like a college campus, with housing like dormitories all over the place. The address I had was for the main building, at the security gate they directed me to it. This was a place where men went to school to become Priest. As I drove up to the building, it looked like a very large cathedral church. I grabbed my tools and put them over my shoulder, and went inside. I saw religious statues, high ceilings, very big stained-glass windows with pretty colors and a red carpet going down a long hallway.

On each side of the hall, there were doors were the priest lived. My customer was in number #105 It was so quiet in the hallway; you could hear a pin drop. I knocked on the door, and a man in a priest attire open the door very slowly, but not all the way. He said, "May I help you?" and I told him "l am a telephone repairman, I'm here to fix your phone". He then told me "oh yes, I am glad you're here, but I am busy right now. Can you come back in about twenty minutes?" and I said "of course, I'll just check your dial tone at the phone terminal to make sure it's in the building." As I was talking to him, I looked over his shoulder into the room. Sitting on a stool, was a little boy, about ten or twelve years old with a choir boy attire, and short pants that matched, looking at me with tears in his eyes and he looked scared. Also, from when he first opens the door, that SMELL hit me, the same smell from the Red-Light District. As I walked away from the door going to the phone terminal, I was totally confused I didn't know why that smell came out that room. Also, why did that boy looked so scared? I knew something was wrong but I couldn't put my finger on it. For one reason, this was way before it came out in the news, that priests were molesting little boys, all over the world, and it was kept quiet for decades. But during that time, it had not come out yet, who knew? I could not get over the fact that something is definitely not right, when I thought about it who would a parent trust their child with the most a doctor, a teacher, and I thought of course a Minister, a Rabbi a Priest these are men of GOD. About five years later on the news, grown men were telling their story, all over the world, on how they were molested when they were a child. People were shocked, I know now what was going on in that room. If I had known then, I would have snatched that kid out that room and called the police. I am sure the kid is grown now, and already told his story. Well, I went and found the phone terminal, and saw that the problem with the customers phone was in the cable outside in the manhole so it was the Cable Departments problem. I went back to tell the priest, knocked on the door a few times, but there was no answer. I left him a note saying his phone will be back on the next day. You don't hear about that on the news like before. I just hope that now that it's been exposed for years maybe it has stop.

Chapter 16

SOMETIMES THERE'S PERKS

On this occasion, I was working late on a Friday evening, and I was dispatched a repair order, which put me into overtime. I didn't mind, because 1. I could use the money, and 2. The address was on Causeway Street at the Boston Garden. I had been to the Boston Garden many times, on my own, to see different events, such as a wrestling match, close circuit boxing Mohamed Ali vs. everyone,(this was before pay preview). I even saw a rodeo and the Harlem Globe Trotters there. I was pretty familiar with the place as a spectator, but this was my first being at the Boston Garden as a worker. At that time, I was working in the Payphone Department.

I knew they had payphones all over the place, and there were a lot of different levels. The Boston Garden was huge, but I was there for one. particular phone number. With my tool belt on my shoulder, and once inside, I started asking the security guards where the phone terminal was. I knew I had to get there first, to know if the dial tone was coming into the building, or if the problem was outside, even before I find the payphone. At that point, the security guards I asked didn't know , and there were people running around all over the place, because there was a game going on, and I kind of got swept up in the crowd. I hadn't gone into the seating area, so I didn't know if it was the Boston Bruins or the Boston Celtics.

All I knew from that point, I had to get a hold of a management personal to show me where that terminal was. So, went over to a Concession Stand and ask to see a manager. The man at the food stand called for me, and said there will be a manager coming to take you where you need to go. After waiting awhile, this guy named Bob came, and took me to the utility room. He then told me, I think the payphone that is out of order is on this floor, but it's all the way around on the other side of the arena. After unlocking the door for me he left. I checked the terminal and found that the dial tone was there, so I was off to the phone on the other side of the arena. It was a very long walk especially with crowds of people all in the way. When I got to the phone, I saw right away what the problem was, the receiver was gone. This happens not all the time, but it does happen, for example, in a bar or a prank at a college. Luckily, I had brought a new receiver with me so I wouldn't have to go back to the phone truck. After replacing the receiver, and hearing dial tone, I called dispatch and closed out the job. It was the last one of the days, and I had been running around like a chicken with his head cut off ever since I entered the building, now I can relax a bit. As I was leaving, I stuck my head in one of the doors where people were seated and cheering, and saw the Boston Celtics playing the Los Angeles Lakers basketball game. Right in front of me were empty seats on the first floor. I was amazed and sat right down and started watching the game for a few minutes, and got caught up in the excitement. It was good to see this, and was unexpected, but I knew I had to get back to the garage and go home, that felt like a nice perk after a busy day.

HOME SWEET HOME, AFTER RETIREMENT FROM THE PHONE COMPANY, I MOVED TO LAS VEGAS TO PURSUE AN ENTERTAINMENT CAREER

Chapter 17

AGAIN SOMETIMES THERE'S PERKS

For some reason, the repair jobs during the week seem ordinary, and then Thursday, Friday, and Saturday comes around, and the repair jobs become strange or just different. I had got a repair job from dispatch, on a Saturday afternoon, to go to an address on Lansdowne Street. I recognized it right away, it was Fenway Park home of the Boston Red Sox. I have been there many times after that day, but this was my first time there so I didn't know where anything was located. So, after parking my phone truck, and grabbing my tools, I went over to the gate everybody else was going through, and told the security guard that I'm with the telephone company, and there are two phones out of order that needs to be put back in service. I need help finding them so the security guard said, "no problem, wait here and I'll get one of the maintenance ground keepers to show you around".

As I was waiting for maintenance, I was watching the people filing into the park by droves. A ball game had just started between the Boston Red Sox and the New York Yankees. People were falling all over themselves trying to get in at all the gates. The maintenance man finally came and said, "you probably want to get into the utility room, and then I can show you where the phones are". I told him that would be great, because this is a big place and I would just be lost in here. The Joe, maintenance man, was an average built Irish man that was really helpful. After we got in the utility room, I checked both phone numbers at the phone terminal and both dial tones were there. I told him we need to go to the phones, and the only description of a location I have is one is in a PRESS BOX, and the other is in a CONDO.

Joe said, "I know where both of those are. One is where the sport casters are, and the other is a room people get together and rent for the day to watch the games, they both are way up overlooking the field". So, we took the elevator up to what they called a condo. It was a large room, with a couch, tables and chairs, a kitchenette type place. with a microwave and a refrigerator. On the other side, was a huge glass window overlooking home plate, and the room stuck out towards the field. It was like you were part of the game, which was going on, and the people down in the seats were screaming and shouting. I had never experienced a ball game from that advantage point. Joe said to me "quite a view , now check this out" he opens the refrigerator, and there was beer and champagne in it, he said "would you like one", I said "no", as I picked up the phone from the table, and there was no dial tone. I traced the long cord back to the phone jack, and realized that someone that had rented the room last, probably was having a good time in the room tripped, and over the cord and pulled it out the phone jack and broke the cord. This was an easy fix once I saw what the problem was. In a big place like this, I always bring extra wires jacks and cords with me, so I don't have to go all the way back to the truck. I called dispatch, and closed out this job. Before I went to the press box, although the two jobs are in the same place, we close them out one at a time.

I asked Joe who was relaxing in one of those comfortable chairs with a cold beverage watching the game, "can you show me how to get to the sport casters booth, this phone is all set". We went down to a long corridor again with hordes of people going in different directions. At one point, I had loss Joe the maintenance man in the crowd, because he was walking kind of fast. I finally caught up with him, and he said, "here we are", it was a wall separating the crowd from the sport casters. I open the door and go in, there were three guys with their headphones on broadcasting the ball game. I said "hi, I am with the telephone company, do you have a phone line out of order?" One of the sports casters turned to me and said, "line three is out" and I said "okay, let me get in there to see what's wrong". Where they were sitting was even closer to the field than the condo room. I had to separate them to get to the wires, which were a tangled mess under the long desk they were sitting at. The phone system they were using at that time was a complex switchboard type, with multiple wires going to different phones. The game was going on, and the sport casters were broadcasting like crazy. To be right there with them, and hearing them doing their thing was amazing! On the floor in that tangle mess of wires, were different connectors, and I had to trace one pair of wires going to one phone line out of twenty, using my ohm meter, and checking for dial tone voltage, which is only forty-eight volts, and tighten the connections that came loose I finally put them back in service. I had them check the lines in between broadcasting, then I called dispatch and closed out the job. Well, I said to them, "you guys are all set", they turned to me and said, "thank you young man! hey why don't you sit down and watch the game" I knew I was at Fenway Park for some time trying to locate everything, and repair the phones, and it was time to head back to the garage and go home. So, I said, "are you sure?" and they said "yeah, this gives you a chance to see how we do this". I have seen these guys on television many times, but to hang out with them for a minute was pretty exciting.

Chapter 18

SNIPPET

Over the years, there were a lot of encounters and situations that I ran into, going from house to house and apartments five to six days a week for over twenty years. Many of which, were small things that happen, but wouldn't make a whole chapter, I call them snippets, and these pages are dedicated to some of them. At one point, after I had been with the phone company a number of years, they decided to change the format, and start charging the customer. What they did, was put an interface connector next to the phone terminal. If the terminal was on a pole, we would put it at wherever the drop wire was going into the building. If the terminal was on the back of the building, we would put it right next to it. If the terminal was in the basement, we then would put the connector next to it. The purpose of the interface was so that if the dial tone was at the interface once we open it up, we knew the problem was in the building somewhere and not outside.

If the problem was inside, we would charge fifty-five dollars an hour to find and repair the service. There was a notice that went out to all the phone company customers that this was the new procedure. One day, I was on my last repair job of the day. I had got to the address, and went straight to the back of a brick building, to the interface connector, and found that the break in the dial tone has to be in the building. It was a four-story apartment building. I went around to the front of the building, and rang the bell, "telephone company" I said, and a lady's voice on the intercom said "come on up, were on the second floor. When I knocked on the door, a middle-aged lady opened the door wide, and said "come on in". I could see the black desk top phone in her living room on a table. There was a middle-aged man sitting on the couch reading a newspaper (which was something people use to do back in the day). So, I told her I checked the wiring outside and I said to the lady "it's okay outside, so the problem with your phone is in here, and if I come in, were going to have to charge you fifty-five dollars an hour to fix the problem." The lady went crazy, she started screaming at her husband "I told you not to call the phone company until we had the money". She then ran over to the phone and snatched it out of the phone jack and went over and hit him right in the side of the head, and he fell out of the couch on to the floor. The lady then ran over to the window and threw the phone out the window, without opening the window, and glass was everywhere . The phone landed two floors down in the middle of the street. It was pure luck it didn't hit anybody. Those black desk top phones were heavy. The lady then started screaming at me. I said, "it looks like you won't have a phone for some time now, but when you're ready to comply and get your service back on call the business office." I turned around and left, but like I said before, when you knock on someone's door or ring their doorbell you never know what mental condition, they are in.

Chapter 19
BOSTON COMMONS

One afternoon I had decided to go back to the garage to have my lunch, and while I was their dispatch gave me my next repair job. They had taken one job away because the customer called back, and said they weren't going to be home and the phone terminal was locked up in the basement, and the maintenance man had left for the day. So, they gave me another repair job which was on Tremont Street across from the Boston Commons. The address was actually called Tremont on the Commons. It was a big luxury condominium with about eight floors overlooking the Commons, which looked like a scale down version of New York Central Park. When I lived in Boston, I always wanted to live there especially with that big, beautiful view of the Boston Commons. There were stores on each side of the condo that went for two hundred yards, a movie theater, and a garage underneath. I parked my phone truck, grabbed my tools out and went in the glass door to the intercoms. The address I was given was Gowdy, with the floor number beside it. I rang the bell, and a female voice said "hello". "Telephone company", I replied, and she said, "come on up". When the elevator door opened, I was in a giant living room, with statues, and paintings, and pictures that were all over the walls. A maid came over to me, and said "have a seat Mr. Gowdy will be with you in a moment", I got up and walked over to the pictures on the wall, there were football greats, baseball greats, the Celtics, and famous boxers, the Boston Bruins.

I thought to myself that this place is awesome, and this guy is really into sports. Then the customer came around the corner stuck his hand out and said, "hi I am Curt Gowdy". I looked at him, and thought to myself whoa what! I have seen him on television many times, he's the voice of the Boston Red Sox, a famous sportscaster. Then surprisingly he said, "I know you, didn't you repair the phones at the sport casting booth in Fenway Park at one of the Red Sox games?" I said, "yes that was me", it was a while back but he remembered. I didn't really pay much attention to the guys in the booth at that time, because of the excitement the game was producing. I told him "I have to go down and get in the utility room and check the phone terminal for dial tone to that specific phone line, which is out of service, he had three different phone lines. After getting into the utility room, I found one side of the wires had come loose. I fixed it and went back up to his condo, and told him to check his phones. "Everything is good" he told me and I asked him "how's the view?" He took me over to a big picture window, and said "take a look." I said, "wow this is amazing" and I said, "well your phone is all set, and it was good seeing you again". Then he said, "wait a minute, I wrote a book about my life and sports would you like a copy?" I said "sure" and he went and got the book and autographed it. I said, "thank you" and left. In this journey as a telephone repairman, once again I never know who I am going to run in to.

Chapter 20

THE COURTYARD

Going back to the beginning, when I became a telephone repair technician, the first thing I heard when I walked into the telephone garage and introduced myself was, "oh so you're the one taking Johnson's place". I said, "yeah, I guess I am the one, so what happen to Johnson?" I asked, and they told me he is in the hospital. "Well, is he sick or in an accident" I asked and they said, "no he was working at a rear wall telephone terminal in a courtyard at the North End of Boston, when he got jumped and beat up, some people thought he was tapping or bugging their phone". "What!" I said, "how is something like that possible, and they said oh it's possible". Well, apparently when they thought some people were doing something illegal, and thought Johnson was investigating their line. They then decided to do something about it. So, the guys at the garage told me whatever you do don't be caught in a courtyard at the North End. Well, I have come full cycle because I have been in those courtyards many of times over the years putting people back in service. I will be getting back to what happened to me one time there later in this book.

So, first being new to the job, I had to go to pole climbing school which was in Braintree Massachusetts. At the time there were two other new people in the garage that had to go to school also. I would pick them up on the way, and bring them back. The school was five days a week for a couple of weeks At that time, it was in January, and about five degrees. We first were inside and the poles were six feet tall. We had to put these straps on our ankles with sharp spikes, that were about two inches long called gaffs. The object was to hold on the pole with one hand, and stick the gaff into the wood, grab the pole with the other hand, and then stick the gaff into the pole, with the other leg and go up the pole. When you have gotten to the top you would then fasten your safety belt around the pole and buckle in. When you have done it successfully, we could then move to the outside poles, which were twenty to thirty feet high and do the same thing until we were comfortable with it. If you're afraid of heights this could be very stressful.

On the last day we had a test, we had to go up to the top of the pole and unbelt ourselves, walk completely around the pole and belt back in. It was about five to ten degrees out, but I was sweating bullets. I had to pass the test because if I didn't , couldn't have the job. Well, I got it done but some people didn't. There was one guy already working for the phone company in the Central Office downtown, but he wanted to be a technician outside. While he was doing the test , his foot gaffed out and that means his gaff didn't go deep enough into the wood, and he slid all the way down the pole to the ground. He was laying on the ground with splinters from the wood sticking out him like a porcupine and blood everywhere. The guy was six feet four and two hundred sixty-five pounds. The trainers ran over to him and said, "lay there were going to call 911 and an ambulance", the guy said "no" and got to his feet, and said "I am going back up there and finish the test because I want this job". Everybody started clapping their hands and applauding him. He then went back up and passed the test, good for him.

After passing pole climbing school, and working in Boston, I found that the telephone poles in the city had iron bars coming out of the poles called steps, and you could grab on and walk up the pole like a latter. Gaffs were not needed on these poles, but everybody that wanted to be an outside technician had to go thru the school, just in case we were in lone country town that didn't have steps on the pole.

Over the years, I have been to the North End of Boston many times. The people there were mostly Italian, always nice and glad to see the telephone man, because they knew I was there to help them get their phone back in service. The North End has some of the best restaurants in Boston, and I enjoyed having lunch there at times. One afternoon, I was dispatched a repair job to go there. The streets there are very narrow, so sometimes with the traffic it would take a while to get to the customer. When I got to the address on Salem Street, I rang the bell. A man opens the door and I said, "hi telephone company" then he introduced himself "I am Angelo Dthomas". The customer was in a hurry to go somewhere, so I told him that to put your phone back in service I would have to get in the courtyard in the back of the building to the phone terminal.

These building are all connected together, and I would have to go through to the kitchen and out the back door to the courtyard. The street behind the customers house was also connected to the same courtyard, so the only way in or out of the yard was thru someone's kitchen. There was one phone terminal for every three buildings in the yard. I told the customer" I'll be back here working on your phone line, and I will let you know what I find". He was a senior gentleman with gray hair and he stood in his kitchen doorway watching me outside in the yard and he said "okay". I found that the problem was in the cable not in his home. I would have to change the pair coming from the Central Office to the terminal box, and put his wires coming from his house to the new wires, and he would be all set. I told him that, and he said, "great and thank you very much" and then he closed the door. As I was working at the terminal, I thought to myself gee I hope he didn't leave. I know he was impatient, so I hurried up and finished the repair job, and called dispatch to have the line tested, and everything was good. I then went over to his back door and knocked, there was no answer. I knocked again, still no answer. I then proceeded to knock a few more times, and call out his name, "Mr. Dthomas are you there? Nothing, now what do I do? I have to get out of this courtyard.

I called my dispatch and told them the predicament I was in, and at first, they laughed. I could hear them telling other people their Bill's locked in a courtyard and can't get out. Well, it wasn't funny to me, then they said it happen before to other technicians you're going to have to knock on a neighbor's door. I really didn't want to do that being a stranger knocking on someone's kitchen back door, but I had no choice. I had to get out of there. So, I thought of an idea, I went to the house right next to my customers so they can see my telephone truck in front of the building and knocked on their door. A man opened the door and said, "may I help you," I showed him my tools and said, "I am with the telephone company and we are here working on the main phone cable because there is a break in the line, and some people are out of phone service like Mr. Dthomas next door". He said "Angelo, yes, I told him, and you can see the phone truck out front, which I have to get to but Angelo has left. Can I get to my truck this way? The guy said, "of course come this way", then I told him "do you mind checking your phones for dial tone". So, he picked up the kitchen phone and said, "yes it's on". So, then I said, "check the other phones, and he checked and told me their all good, and thank you for keeping our service on". As I was moving through the kitchen towards the front of the house, he said "we were about to eat why don't you sit down and join us", there was a whole family getting ready to have dinner. I said, "no I have to get going" and he thanked me again even the little kids said thank you Mr. Phone Man.

When I got back to my truck, I couldn't help thinking about my first day at the telephone garage. When the guys told me what happen to the other technician in the courtyards here, well at least I didn't get beat up, and I met some nice people.

I PERFORMED IN MOST OF THE CASINOS, BRINGING HAPPINESS AND JOY TO PEOPLE, SINGING OLDIES BUT GOODIES, FOR THE BABY BOOMERS.

Chapter 21

THE ROOKIE

I was in the phone company garage one early morning, when my foreman came to me and said, "how would you like a new guy, a rookie, to ride with you today?" "You know train him, show him the ropes, just for today to see if he would like the job". I said "sure". I figured it would be good having some company and someone to talk to for a change. Normally, we repair technicians are all alone in the truck all day. Which is good, because you are your own boss.

The rookie was a young, black, kid in his twenties name Jimmy. At this point, I had been a repair technician for over ten years, so I had plenty of experience putting people's phones back in service. This was a nice kid, and I explained to him that we have to go to the first job, that I got from dispatch, and then we can take a break. I never know how long a particular repair job is going to take, it could be one hour or three hours, so we have to get that first one out of the way. We arrived at the customers apartment building, and got out the truck. I told him we could go ring the bell, and check for dial tone inside, but I wanted to show him the phone terminal at the back of the building, which was on the wall in the back yard.

I told Jimmy "if the phone terminal was on a pole, then I might have checked inside first, because the problem could be in there, and I wouldn't have to put all the gear on to climb a pole which is more work". After finding the customers dial tone at the terminal, we went around front and rang the bell, Before the customer answered the door, I told Jimmy to "watch what I do, you have to be pleasant and professional at the same time". The customer was on the first floor, he opens the door and he was a middle aged, Caucasian man, and he was pissed off. He started yelling at us saying his phone had been out for three days and that he needed his phone for his business, and that he was tired of this shit. "Well," I said to him, I am sorry he had to wait that long, but I am here to help him. I said to the customer, "my coworker and I will have you back in business in no time". Meanwhile, I notice Jimmy, who was standing beside me, when the door opened, was now behind me and shaking, as I glanced to see where he was.

We went in and I started checking the phone jacks, beginning with the kitchen wall phone because that's normally where the dial tone comes in from the outside. As I took the phone off the wall, I saw that some wires were broken, from the customer slamming the receiver down hard when he hanged up the phone, and that made the wires loose and break in the wall, which is an easy fix. This is something that doesn't happen a lot, but slam hard enough it happens. Once the connection is broken there, the rest of the jacks in the house won't work.

I showed Jimmy, and then the customer, and he said, "I was angry at a lot of people the last few weeks, and I guess I must have been slamming the phone down to hard". Then he said, "I am sorry for yelling at you guys, it's just been a terrible time for me". Then he said, "would you guys like some beer, soda or water?" I replied, "no were all set". Then he thanked us, for putting him back in service. When we got back to the phone truck, Jimmy said "wow, that guy was acting like a crazy man, he scared me, but you calmed him right down. I thought he was going to hit us with something!" I told Jimmy it takes a while but you get use to some people getting mad because their phone is out of service. You will start to understand how to talk to them, and put their mind at ease once they know that you are there to help them and everything will be alright.

Chapter 22

THE ROOKIE

After the first repair job in the morning, we took a break. At McDonalds, for a breakfast sandwich, and coffee. Jimmy the trainee had a lot of questions, such as what if the guy did this or what if the guy did that? From what he was asking me, he was scared of getting hurt by an irate customer. Basically, I told him eighty to ninety percent of the people we see as telephone repair men and women, are nice and kind people. I told Jimmy with the training and patience; it gets easier in time. It was still early in the morning, and we had a long day ahead

The next two jobs were pretty normal. We got to a customer's house, and he was not at home. I told Jimmy "we still have to check for dial tone at the phone terminal", and in this case it was on a pole, in the alley, in back of the house. Jimmy had not been scheduled for pole climbing school yet. It was to be in two weeks. But since he had some time before the school starts, the phone company wanted him to ride with an experience technician, to see if it's something he really wants to do. So, after I pulled the phone truck down the alley, I put my climbing gear on, and went up the pole to the terminal, explaining everything I was doing, to jimmy on the ground. The dial tone was not there, which meant that there was a ground on the line, (a naked wire touching metal) or a break in the line from the terminal to the Central Office, where the dial tone comes from. We have a meter to measure where the problem is in the cable, then call the Central Office, and change the wires to a new line. We call that getting a spare pair, to get the customer dial tone. I explained all this to Jimmy, as I was doing it, this took a lot of time, but I knew when the customer came home that night, they would be happy the phone was back on. Our next repair job was at an Italian restaurant, in the North End of Boston. When we got there, we pulled up in front, so the manager saw us and came over to greet us. As he opens the door, with a big smile on his face he said, 'boy I am so glad you guys are here! guess you want to get to the phone terminal out back?" I replied, "yes, we will start there", then he said, "follow me". As we walked through the back of the restaurant, I picked up a couple of desk phones to check for dial tones. When we got out back it was a courtyard, and the terminal was near his back door. The manager said, "just come on in when you're finished", "okay" I said and started checking the lines. I was showing Jimmy how to do that, and found that the problem was in the restaurant. As we were going from phone jack to phone jack, the owner came over to me and said, "we had a spill in the kitchen the other day, would that have anything to do with the phone being off?" I went and checked a connection in the kitchen near the floorboards, and though they had wiped the spill up, the wires at the connection jack had shorted out. After I open up the box, and cleaned off the wires, and put on a new jack, all the phones were working again. The owner said to us "thank you very much!" "now sit down so that we can feed you guys!" I said, "no that's alright", but he kept insisting, "you guys did me a big favor, and I want to show my appreciation".

I want to treat you to a great Italian dinner", the manager said. Normally we don't accept gratuities but it was around lunch time anyway, so I said to Jimmy "what the heck". Then the owner said to the waiters, "give the phone men whatever they want". The manager came over to me with a big smile, and said "before you leave, you have got to take some cannoli's home, for dessert they are the best in the North End". After we left that customer, in the phone truck Jimmy said, "you know, that was pretty good", and I replied "yeah, you have to take the good with the bad, and most repair jobs are not that bad". Jimmy and I had another normal repair job, and then we were at the last job of the day. It was a four-story apartment building in the South End of Boston, on Tremont Street, not too far from where I use to live. The customer was a Mrs. Davis on the third floor. From the work order, I knew the phone terminal was in the back of the building, down an alley so we went there first, and everything was okay there and the line going into the house looked good, so we went around front. I ranged the bell and through the intercom, a lady's voice said, "who is it?", "telephone company" I replied, "come on up third floor" she replied. When we got up there, she opens the door yelling, something I have heard before many times, why is it always my phone that's out?

The lady looked like she was in her forties, average size with brown hair, but the difference with this customer, was she was holding a leash with a huge red Doberman dog on the end of it. The dog was barking and snarling at us. At that moment Jimmy screamed and took off running down the stairs. I said to the lady, "we are not coming in your apartment with this dog barking at us, the problem with your phone seems to be inside, and we are here to help you get back in service". Then she said, "okay I'll put the dog away so you can come in", so I told her "I have to get some more tools, and my coworker, and I will be right back", she said "leave the door open downstairs so you can get back in". Well, went back downstairs, and Jimmy was sitting in the truck. Apparently, he didn't lock the door when he got out, and I have the keys. The first thing he said to me was "I can't do this", so "I said to him, it's not always like this, come on back up there with me so I can find the problem fix it and close out this job. She has put the dog away, Jimmy then said are you sure, Bill that dog was mean, yeah but he's not going to hurt us". I finally talked Jimmy to come back upstairs, with me, when she opens the door, we could still hear that dog barking away. I told her were going to start with the kitchen phone, and go room to room until we fix the problem. She seemed nicer this time, and Jimmy was more at ease.

The dial tone at the kitchen wall phone was there, which means there is a broken wire in the living room or one of the bedrooms. I put my buzzer on her kitchen jack, and started tracing the wires from one room to another. While in one of the bedrooms, Jimmy asked "can we close the door, I know that dog is in another room, but he still sounds like he wants to rip us apart". "I said your right yeah close it" I was tracing the wires with my probe along the base boards, I came to a phone jack behind a dresser that had been chewed off by the dog. I took the jack apart and could hear my buzzer loud and clear and the dial tone.

put a new jack on, then went to open the door to tell Mrs. Davis what the problem was and the dog was right there at the door snapping at me and I slammed the door, Jimmy said "what the f—k, we got to get out of here!" I cracked the door open, and yelled for Mrs. Davis three times, before she answered. I replied, I said "your phone is all fixed, can you please come get your dog, so we can leave. We were both yelling, and I heard her say "come here King". The dog went to her, and she grabbed him by his leash, and started walking towards us. As I was trying to explain to her what happen to the phone jack in that room, her whole attitude changed. She started screaming saying "my phone should have been fix days ago!" The dog still barking, then she said, "I should sic my dog on you". At that point, Jimmy took off again, we weren't too far from the front door. I was nervous, but I stood my ground, knowing that yeah it was a big Doberman but it wasn't a Pit Bull which I had for six years. I told her "we came and put you back in service and you shouldn't have any more problems, and that you didn't need to threaten us with your dog, which I am going to put in my report when I talk to dispatch". "Hopefully nothing else is going to happen, but if it does, you may have a hard time getting someone back here to work on your phone line especially if the problem is in your apartment, knowing you have a huge Doberman that you want to sic on people!" After that, I told her have a nice day and left.

When I got back to the truck, Jimmy was sitting in the truck rocking back and forth shaking his head, and he said, "I am not going to do this!" He told me, "you have a way of talking to people, calming them down and being polite. If they are in my face like that, I am not going to be able to take it". I told Jimmy that the job pays good with good benefits and with the phone truck, it's like you are your own boss. So, after our last job of the day, we went back to the garage. My foreman Bob came over to me and asked, "when Jimmy went into the break room, did he like the job?", I said "no, he can't handle talking to the customers, and dogs really scares him". The Foreman replied, "well did you tell him about the benefits and the pay raises?" I told Bob, "yes I did, but he didn't want to hear it", and Bob said, "well we tried, the jobs not cut out for everyone". I personally felt bad for Jimmy, he was a nice kid. About seven years later, I went into a McDonald's and Jimmy was behind the counter. I didn't recognize him at first, he had gain weight, but he saw me and said, " hey Bill how's it going?" So, we got to talking, and he told me he had gotten married, but his wife got laid off, and he wasn't making enough money to make ends meet. Then he asked me "are the phone company hiring, because am ready now". I told him "as far as I know they weren't, but he could go down to the phone company employment office and apply, because there might be other positions available". After I got my food, I told him good luck and left. I often wondered what happen to him after that, and how he made out. One thing I found in life, through experience, is that you have to grab opportunity, when you have a chance because it may not come around ever again.

SNIPPET #2

Here we have another unusual repair job, it was on a Monday afternoon. I received a service order to go to an address by the Feins which were some streets next to Fenway Park, where the Boston Red Sox play. That area also had a beautiful garden covering a city block, with pretty flowers, which people would walk thru and admire. When I got to the address, I went straight to the phone terminal at the back of the building, and checked for the customers dial tone and it was there.

I then went around front and rang the customer's bell. A lady's voice said "hello", and I said, "Mrs. Butler it's the phone company", she said "come on in." I knew from the repair order ; she was on the second floor. I went upstairs, and she open the door, she a middle-aged, average built, Italian woman, and she started complaining right away as I walked into her apartment. "Why is it always my phone that's out of order?" I said to her, like always do, "well I am here to help you get back in service". Then she said, "because nobody came out to fix my phone quick enough, I called the president of the phone company and he said he'll send someone out right away".

This happens now and then with irate customers that don't have any patience, they go all the way up the chain of command to the president and demand results. I think he must be tired of people calling his office all the time, so he tells them what they want to hear to get them off the phone. The lady had two different phone numbers. She had a kitchen wall phone that was working, and a desk phone on the kitchen table that she was pointing to, and yelling that phone is out of order. I picked up the phone and there was no dial tone, so I went down under the table to the phone jack, and to my surprise the phone wasn't plugged in. So, I said "there's the problem the phones not plugged in". I plugged it in and picked up the phone, and it was working. Then all of a sudden, the lady ran up to me screaming at me and said, "if the phone was unplugged, then YOU UNPLUGED IT!"

Wait , What? At that moment, a television show hosted by Rod Sterling went through my head. I could hear the music, am I in the TWILIGHT ZONE? Then her wall phone rang, and she went over and picked it up and turned around and said, "do you know a Bob Smith?" I said, "yes that's my foreman", now I am thinking good timing and as she handed me the phone, I said "hello" then Bob said, "Bill gets out of there the woman has been calling the phone company all day she's CRAZY!" I said, "yeah you can say that again!" I turned to start picking up my tools, and I handed her the phone, Bob had hung up. and I told her, "your phone is all set", and she was still yelling as I left. I thought had seen it all but that was a new one!

SNIPPET 3
NORTHEASTERN UNIVERSITY

Over the years, I had a lot of repair jobs at different colleges, and there were quite a few in Boston, MA. There was Wentworth Institute, Boston University, Boston College, University of Massachusetts, and in Cambridge MA. there was M.I.T. and Harvard University. I repaired telephones in all those places and more. One of the repair jobs that sticks out, was at Northeastern University. It was on a Saturday, about mid-afternoon, and I received a repair order to go there on Huntington Avenue. The repair order was at a radio station, inside the university, and I had to search around to find it. The college was big, so I got directions from different people, until finally got to the hallway with the glass windows. There were famous singers, with their pictures on the walls, and as I approached one of the widows, saw the disc jockey that was talking and playing music that I was hearing in the halls and on the radio in the phone truck.

That radio station was very popular and played all over Boston and Cambridge MA. When I walked into the DJ Room, she took the headphones off and said, "hi I'm D". She knew who I was because of my tool belt draped over my shoulder. I said, "hi I'm Bill, so one of your phone lines is out of order," she showed me on her big switchboard, which line it was. She put her headphones back on and went back on the air She started talking and playing music. But as I looked around the room, there were hundreds of cable and phone wires going everywhere. I knew it was going to be hard tracing that one line, that was out among all of that mess of wires all over the floor. I had gone to the phone terminal, and her dial tone was there, so I put my beeper on that phone line and was on the floor trying to find it. So, while the songs were playing, she was talking to me and on the air, she told her listeners "we have a phone line out and Bill the phone man is here and nice enough to be looking for the problem".

Then she started asking me questions, "are you married, how long you been with the phone company, you look like you work out?" It was just conversation, the wires were hanging off the table she was sitting at and I told her "l have to go under the table to trace these wires", she said "okay", then I heard her say over the air "Bill is now under my desk working", then she said "oooww Bill stop that tickles", when she said that it startled me and my head hit the bottom of the table. Of course, she was only kidding, I hadn't touched her legs and she had pants on. I finally found the problem, one of the connection equipment splicers had come loose. I got up and told her to check that line, she said, "yes the dial tone is back on" and she stood up with a big smile and shook my hand and thanked me. She was really a nice person, with a great personality. I couldn't help thinking about her for the rest of the day, besides she was on my radio. When I got back to the phone garage, I was besieged by my fellow workers, with a lot of questions. Bill, we know that was you at the radio station what did she look like? Was she pretty? Were you really between her legs? Did you ask her out? I was single, and told them "no I didn't ask her out, but maybe I should have she looked great".

SNIPPET #4
THE BLIND LADY:

One afternoon, I received another repair order for the South End of Boston. It was on Tremont Street, and exactly around the corner from where I lived. It was a brick apartment building with five floors, that held the elderly and low-income people. It was my last repair job on a Friday, and according to the repair order, the phone terminal was in the basement. I rang the customers bell, Miss Woods in apartment #302, she said "hello" I told her "it's the phone company, and I have to get to the basement, then I'll be up to see you" she said "okay". When I got to the terminal, I saw that her dial tone was not there. Normally in this case, I would find a spare pair of wires, by going back to the Central Office we call "tip and ring". The dial tone comes from the office on one side, to the terminal the 'tip", and goes back to the Central Office on the other side the "ring". But there were no spare pairs available. I had to call dispatch, and tell them to give it to the Cable Department, and they would repair the problem in the manhole. However, dispatch told me the Cable Department was all booked up solid until Monday, and this was Friday. So that meant that the customer would have to be out of service the whole weekend. I went upstairs to tell Miss Woods that her phone would be back on Monday. I knocked and she open the door and said, "please come in", as I was walking in explaining to her the situation. She kind of walked into a chair, and said to me "1 can't wait until Monday, I am blind and have a heart problem".

She then told me she has emergency response on speed dial, and she needs her phone on because she has to have help a couple time a week and she lives alone. My heart went out to her, this was an older lady in her eighties how could I leave her with no communication the whole weekend. I knew I just had to help her so told her "1 am not supposed to do this, but I am going to get you dial tone just for the next few days". put my buzzer on her line at her phone jack and traced it down at the terminal, and then took her wires off her binding post, and put them on someone else's binding post that had dial tone it. A binding post is what we wrap the wires around coming from the apartments. There was a lot of apartments in the building, and the Cable Department would be able to put her back online once they repaired the problem in the manhole. I went back to Miss Woods, took my buzzer off her jack, and said "listen you have dial tone now, but it's not your dial tone it's one of your neighbors, so if the phone rings DO NOT PICK IT UP!" "If you really have to make a call, and you hear someone talking, hang up quickly until their done". I told her "this is only for a few days and she will be back in business". She was very grateful, and said, "you are a life saver "and thanked me. I said, "your welcome and goodbye" and then I left. I was hoping that I had did a good deed in case of an emergency.

SNIPPET 5
CO-ED

I was, at the time, in the Payphone Department. This happened on a nice Spring day when I received a repair order to fix a payphone at Northeastern University on Huntington Avenue. I have been to this college many times before. This job was in one of the dormitories. I went to the office on the first floor, and I asked the guy at the desk "where was the payphone that was out of order?", and he told me "it was on the second floor halfway down the hallway". I got to the second floor, and it was like most college dormitories, students running all around up and down in the hallways. But there was something different here. I have repaired phones in the boy's dormitories and the girl's dormitories, but here were girls and boys on the same floor. I didn't really pay much attention though because I was focus on the job at hand trying to get this payphone to work. After going down to the basement to the phone terminal, and back to the payphone, I finally got it to work. Before I leave, I had to use to the men's room. I saw a door that said men on it, but the metal letters that said men were gone off the door and all that was left was the outline. So, I peeked in, and there were the urinals, so I knew I was in the right place. As I was using the bathroom doing number one, a girl came in and said, "hi how's it going", it shocked me, so I got closer to the urinal. She was oh so cheerful, and went into a stall and closed the door, and could hear her using the toilet, and then she said this, "it's such a nice day outside I hope it doesn't rain what do you think?"

I answered her saying "yes, it is", as zipped up as fast as I could without catching myself in my fly and ran out the bathroom. I headed back down to the office thinking WHAT THE F K! I went to the office and told the guy at the desk what happen and he said, "oh yeah it's all co-ed now, you can see we took the letters off the men and women's restrooms", and I said , "yeah, I saw that on the door but I never experience that before", he said "yeah, all the colleges are doing that now". Now that was back before cell phones, and I know times have changed a lot. Nowadays, they even have restrooms to go in if you don't consider yourself man or woman. I have repaired telephones in different colleges since then but, I just haven't seen or experienced anything like that anymore. I haven't talked to any students about that particular situation, so I don't know if they still implementing the co-ed thing or they went back to how it was before, because I could see some problems arising from that policy!

The Authors Notes

Whatever your situation, and you know in your heart, you will get great results if you stick with it, and then don't give up. If it's being a cook, dancer, singer, an entertainer, an artist, a doctor, a lawyer, or excel in sports, just don't give up. No matter what I went through, I had to persevere, and be professional, so I could earn a paycheck. A lot of times, I had to bite my tongue, and not act belligerent like some of the people did that I was trying to help. Most of the people were kind and nice, but over the years, I had come across some that weren't.

So going through life you have to be kind, and treat people with respect, even if you're not getting respect back. There were days I wanted to quit, but my intestinal fortitude, and asking God what should I do? , made me stay and I am glad I did. The experience I received associating with different people from all cultures, creeds, races and economic levels cannot be put in words.